Authentic Leader

Strength through Empathy,
Vulnerability and other Insights

AMAL CANDIDO

Copyright © 2020

All rights reserved. No portion of the book may be reproduced or utilized in any form or by any means, electronic or mechanical, including photocopying, recording, or by any other information storage and retrieval system, without permission in writing from the author.

Dedication

To my mom. You've inspired me so much to be who I am today. Your resilience and perseverance amid pain, struggles and uncertainty has no bounds. Your humility and sacrifice in all that you have done to provide for your children is a true testament and a great example to a mother's love. I am forever grateful and internally changed by all the hardship you have faced to continue moving forward in life. Your unconditional love, your unshaken faith and your vulnerabilities have inspired me deeply and touched my heart. Your love is beyond what words can describe; I can only hope to come close to being the great woman that you are! I am blessed and changed because of you. Love you forever, Mom.

To my son. Nicholas, you make me so proud to be your mom. You have grown into a wonderful young man with a compassionate heart, a great sense of humor, and a passion that will carry you well through life. Every day I spend with you is always the best day ever! I am blessed to have you as my son. You've taught me all about Transformers, Pokémon and Yokai Watch. Nothing in life is as rewarding as being part of your life and watching you grow. You are my heart, my light, and my love!

To my husband. We have been through a lot of ups and downs. I'm not one to say more of the lows than the high times in life, but I must admit there is no one else I want to be with in this unsettled, rocky journey than you. You push me to my limits, because you believe in me more than I believe in myself. You see my strength and what I can do before I even see it in myself. You have seen the flaws, the hurts, and the brokenness in me, and yet you are still here. How many relationships work so well when one has fallen and the other is always there to give comfort and support? It's not great timing how that worked out. It's knowing when to stop and to lean into the struggles to make the other a priority, until we are both back on solid ground together. Agape love at its finest! Thank you for loving me even when it's hard to "love the unlovable." I am deeply touched by the forgiveness, love, courage, and vulnerability you have shown me.

Contents

PART 1: HOW TO EMBRACE EMPATHY & EMOTIONAL INTELLIGENCE 9

Chapter 1: *Empathy Is An Important Quality, But Is It A Trait Or A Skill?* 11

Chapter 2: *Three Core Leadership Qualities Needed To Make A Positive Change* 17

Chapter 3: *Four Stages Of Learning Emotional Intelligence* .. 21

Chapter 4: *Learning & Developing Emotional Intelligence* 25

PART 2: LEADERSHIP THAT MATTERS 33

Chapter 5: *Reflecting On Your Leadership: If It Isn't Broken, Then Break It* 35

Chapter 6: *Leadership – What Gets In The Way Of Building An Engaged Team?* 41

Chapter 7: *Leadership: Team Management – Turn An Ordinary Team Into A Hot Team* 51

Chapter 8: *Tips For Managers On Trusting Employees* 57

PART 3: LEARNING & IMPROVING YOURSELF 61

Chapter 9: *Why A Mentoring Connection Is So Important?* ... 63

Chapter 10: *Overcoming Obstacles To Success* 69

Chapter 11: *Transparency – Don't Make It Personal, And You Will Thrive!* 75

Chapter 12: *Employee Evaluation: Measuring Intangible Traits* 81

Chapter 13: *Mistakes You're Probably Making When Scheduling A Meeting* 87

Chapter 14: *How To Design Meetings That Your Team Will Enjoy And Attend* 91

PART 4: EVERYTHING IN BETWEEN 95

Chapter 15: *Agility – What Does It Mean And Why Should You Care?* 97

Chapter 16: *The Importance Of Strategy In Employer Branding* 103

PART 5: THE TOXIC WORK ENVIROMENT 111

Chapter 17: *A Toxic Work Culture And How To Change It* 113

Chapter 18: *Workplace Cultures: Toxicity After A Merger* ..119

Chapter 19: *What Do You Expect If Your Executive Wears Multiple Masks And Is Toxic?* 125

Introduction

I have been working for years, through high school and beyond. I was also a stay-at-home mom until it was time to put away the small toys and no longer live behind the toddler world.

Who knew that I would face biases of my own returning to the workforce after seven years, trying to convince people that I have great skills and I would like to put them into good use? It took a lot of hard work, but perseverance won, and I was ready to make the leap back in! I wanted to work with real adults and have professional conversations, using big people words! Now my work-life balance life has begun…with managing new learnings and new challenges professionally, while keeping life balance in check. Juggling home and work life has always been a delicate balance for women to maintain. It is never easy, but it has its rewards.

Now you see, I've always had an issue with separating the work-life balance "thing" when it comes to the bigger picture. You work because you have to, and you live a life at home because you want to spend time with the people you love. It's the splitting of these that I am not convinced can be done 100%, because I believe we all bring our whole self to work whether we like to admit it or not. Work is essential to building our careers. It's that part of our lives that activates passion, creativity and a sense of accomplishment.

With that, my takeaway and learned lesson is that I need certain things from home to make my day at work easier to manage. Specifically, I need three fundamental things: mindfulness, self-reflection, and faith (or whether you want to call it, maybe hope or strength).

Mindfulness will give you the clarity to see things as they are, on the inside and outside of yourself. This clarity will help clear out the clutter and the noise around you and help you grow to be the person you were meant to be.

Self-reflection is key to living a fulfilled life, as it takes your mind off comparing your life with others around you. It will bring you to focus on your "self" to be able to answer key questions along your journey such as, am I on the right path? [your career] Who do I want to be? [your legacy] what do I want to do? [your goals or accomplishments] Where do I need to go? [your compass, your northern star, or direction]

What I know for sure is this: as much as I despise uncertainty, and even though change magnifies my fears, they both played a big role in my journey personally and professionally. I was able to learn that open-mindedness will get me far in life. Having a growth mindset is crucial to succeeding whether personally or professionally. I have not completely mastered those two areas of my life. I am a work-in progress for sure, having yet to embrace uncertainty and change as I have always been the person who plans, and follows a to-do list. That's how I measured my own success and accomplishments in general. To that end, the best advice I have ever received is to live life with intention, to hope and press through the challenges to believe in myself, to take a pause to allow for self-reflection and to live with mindfulness in order to be who I need to be.

Amal

PART 1:

HOW TO EMBRACE EMPATHY & EMOTIONAL INTELLIGENCE

Chapter 1

Empathy Is An Important Quality, But Is It A Trait Or A Skill?

We all hear about empathy, whether at work, church, school, or with family members in our daily interactions.

I don't know about you, but recently, the topic of empathy comes up quite often. I worked for an executive who used to have a lot of discussion around empathy to his team and how important it is in doing business with clients and when managing others.

I also attended a 3-hour workshop on emotional intelligence and read a lot of business articles on the topic. The most common theme I've found is that successful leaders usually have empathy as one of their top soft skills in business and in managing their employees.

Empathy resonates with me, and it is a big part of who I am as a person. The ability to understand others and to think outside of oneself, being able to relate to different people and their hardships or whatever their feelings might be, is something I try to experience daily. I get intentional about it and seek scenarios or people who might need some empathy to touch their hearts and to build a connection with them. On a personal level, I find that I like the person I become when I am experiencing empathy, whether receiving or extending it on to others.

Speaking for myself, I have been in many difficult situations, where I truly believe God put amazing people in my life to help me through a tough/challenging experience. Every time I had the opportunity to extend empathy to others, I felt my heart swell and grow larger. I have this sense of joy and profound gratitude, which is hard for me to explain in words, other than to say it was amplified through feelings and emotions.

One might ask, what is the definition of empathy? In a simple google search, empathy is the ability to share someone else's feelings or experiences by imagining what it would be like to be in that person's situation.

So, does it mean that empathy can be a skill?

Daniel Goleman, the author of the book *Emotional Intelligence*, says, "Empathy is the ability to understand others' emotions." Empathy is a skill that can be developed and, as with most interpersonal skills, empathizing (at some level) comes naturally to most people.

Ok, so now is empathy a skill or a trait?

Empathy is a complex suite of skills that builds upon itself. While reflexive empathy is an inborn trait, it does not automatically lead to the cognitive empathy required to build and sustain meaningful relationships, hold a job, or parent a child effectively (Jan 15, 2014, by Nebraska children).

How can a person demonstrate empathy toward others?

To be empathic, you must think beyond yourself and your concerns. Once you see beyond your world, you'll realize there's so much to discover and appreciate! You can start by doing the following:

- Putting aside your viewpoint
- Validating the other person's perspective
- Listening attentively
- Responding with encouraging messages
- Asking what the other person would do. When in doubt, ask the person to explain his or her position. This is probably the simplest and most direct way to understand the other person. However, it's perhaps the least used way to develop empathy.

Is empathy a learned behavior?

Empathy is a learned behavior even though the capacity for it is inborn. You can increase your empathy by doing the following:

- Challenging yourself
- Getting out of your usual environment
- Asking better questions
- Getting feedback
- Walking in another's shoes
- Examining your biases
- Getting curious
- Exploring the heart of another, not just the mind (this may be the most important)

The capacity for empathy varies from one person to the next. Not surprisingly, the extent of your emotional intelligence plays a critical factor in the following:

- Knowing what you're feeling
- Accurately labeling and naming different emotions with precision
- Using your feelings to inform your thinking

The more connected you are to your own emotions, the greater your ability to feel for others. Again, once you realize that empathy has a cognitive component, this makes perfect sense. It should come as no surprise that research shows adolescents who consider friendships and social connections as important, and are "embedded" in their social networks, are more likely to display empathy than those who don't and believe themselves to be outsiders.

Emotional intelligence is the ability to identify and manage your own emotions and the emotions of others. It is generally said to include three skills:

- Emotional awareness
- The ability to harness emotions and apply them to tasks like thinking and problem solving
- The ability to manage emotions, which includes regulating your own emotions and cheering up or calming down other people

To sum up, the key point is that developing an empathic approach is the most significant effort you can make toward improving your people skills. When you understand others, they will probably want to understand you, and this is how you can start to build cooperation, collaboration, and teamwork.

Self-paced exercise

1. What are the physical symptoms you experience with emotion? (An example might be your face turns red when you are angry).

2. How did you learn to recognize or manage your emotions? What about learning to recognize what other people are feeling and going through?

3. What is a fundamental change you might like to make now that you know change can happen at a physical level? What would you like to train your brain to do?

4. What will make practicing EQ skills the most challenging for you?

Quick, in-the-moment questions to ask yourself (Craig Ferguson):

➢ Does this need to be said?

➢ Does this need to be said by me?

➢ Does this need to be said now?

Here are some fascinating findings to consider:

- Your EQ tends to increase with age.

- The most significant EQ gap between Baby Boomers and Generation Y (Millennials) is in their self-management skills.
- Women and men have the same average self-awareness score, while men score higher in self-management, and women score higher in social awareness and relationship management.
- CEOs and other senior executives, on average, have the lowest EQ scores in the workplace.

Chapter 2

Three Core Leadership Qualities Needed To Make A Positive Change

Good leaders help guide us. They make the tough calls that keep organizations, companies, and countries moving forward. Determining whether moving forward is beneficial or harmful depends on the leader's ability to recognize if their actions will impact others in a beneficial or detrimental way.

We can spot a lousy leader almost immediately. Our society has proven quite adept at this. The question here is, can we spot a good leader, and what is it exactly that would make a good leader? Positive leadership requires *action* (focus), provides *direction* (vision), and *inspires* (character).

Focus

The first core leadership quality is focus. Self-awareness means being able to look within oneself and listen to your inner voice. Those who heed their inner voice ultimately make better decisions, as they will use this connection with their "real self" to elicit resources or to gain clarity in decision making. It is a concept not easily explained, so let's dive into an example here.

Pay careful attention to your body's internal signals. These are physiological changes that are very subtle; your brain notices them with concentration. This area of your brain tucked behind your frontal lobes is known as the insula. Sit still and tune into the insula by focusing on your heartbeat. With practice, you will recognize this and other "stories" your body tells you.

Vision

The second core leadership quality is **vision**. Make a draft of your goal(s). Share with others. Refine it using feedback and support your vision with commitment and inspiration that moves you personally.

Now, try it out with colleagues. Ask your colleagues/team to create a vision and share it. This will build trust as you discover how to capitalize on what drives each individual and use strength in diversity as a significant competence.

Communication is the ultimate key to these qualities' success. Having a positive delivery, placing a high value on two-way communication, often meeting if needed, over-communicating, and choosing the right words by knowing your audience will support your vision.

Character

The third core leadership quality is **character**. Respectfulness of others and your beliefs, fairness, cooperation, compassion, and humility are the traits you use to bring out this skill.

The self-discipline and courage of taking action on your vision, and the passion used to achieve acceptance of your goals, brought forth by the wisdom and competence gained from experience will be used to transform the strength of your leadership.

The social conscience of your leadership character is developed by being mindful of your integrity, honesty, loyalty, and selflessness as a leader.

Final thoughts

Leaders more accustomed to giving input rather than being attentive will have trouble with any of the above. Be wary of any "noise" that distracts the path to achieving your vision. Leaders who stay true to their values are known to succeed better in the long run.

You must believe in and practice these three leadership qualities and be aware that the outcome will benefit yourself, those around you, and others you may not meet without negative impact or consequences.

Self-paced exercise

Practice statements that you can use start with "I." (the Sling Team)

- I am comfortable making important decisions with plenty of lead time.
- I am comfortable making important decisions with no lead time.
- I do not blame others for my problems.
- I am approachable even during stressful times.
- I have a positive attitude in the face of adversity.

A good example of a chart of leadership qualities that a leader may possess:

Qualities/Characteristics	Skills/Abilities
A leader can - assume responsibility - take initiative A leader is - achievement-orientated - adaptable to situations - alert to social environment - assertive - competent - cooperative - courageous (risk-taker) - decisive (good judgment) - dedicated (committed) - dependable - energetic (high activity level) - enthusiastic - honest (high integrity) - optimistic - persistent - self-confident - tolerant of stress or anxiety (resilient)	A leader can - communicate well - listen openly to others - resolve conflict A leader is - broad-minded (seeks diversity) - clever (intelligent) - conceptually skilled (holistic view) - creative (imaginative) - diplomatic and tactful - extraverted (outgoing) - fair-minded (just) - forward-looking (vision) - knowledgeable about team/group tasks - motivational (inspirational) - organized - persuasive (influential) - socially skilled - technically skilled - well-spoken (good speaker)

Chapter 3

Four Stages Of Learning Emotional Intelligence

I believe emotional intelligence can be gained or improved upon at any point in life. The real question to ask is, do we think we have the right environment to learn and practice emotional intelligence skills? Do we need to have a resourceful environment to enable us to see the areas or the aspects of EI that we should work on, and to seek understanding and ask for expert advice on how to do so? Based on some reading of my own, there are four stages of learning EI: insight, assessment, training, and lastly, application.

Let's dive at a high-level onto each stage to see how it all comes together.

Insight

Having insight that something in us needs either changing or improving is the first important step. We must recognize a need in us to reach our full potential. Any learning starts when there is awareness; once it identifies, the next step is to ask ourselves, are we ready to make those changes?

With emotional intelligence, there are crucial components that are worth discovering, such as the following:

Self-awareness – Understanding how we are feeling, and why we feel this way.

Self-regulation – Our ability to express our feelings in a way that does not make us look like fools by being overly emotional, lashing out, etc.

Motivation – What moves us internally? Our drives and passions impact how we want to change, how we express ourselves and how we want to live life.

Empathy – The ability to understand and share the feelings of another and seeing the world from their perspective. It's not as much about solving someone's problem as it is about truly being there, supporting, and offering encouraging words.

Social skills – The ability to communicate effectively, build strong relationships, and connect, whether personally or professionally, which are equally important. Gaining insights into which aspects we need to work on is key. Some of us might be excellent communicators with strong social skills but lack self-regulation.

This is a skill that I am all too familiar with, as I work with my son to help him express his disappointments, hurts and losses while balancing what he gains in life experience with a hopeful outlook, no matter what the situation looks from the inside.

The learning process starts with knowing which aspect of emotional intelligence needs to be developed and focused on, so you are off to a good start.

Assessment

There are many tests widely available online to help you measure where you stand on each EI aspect. I've listed a few links below for you to try. Some are free; however, if you would like a full report, it's available at a fee:

MindTools – https://www.mindtools.com/pages/article/ei-quiz.htm

Emotional Intelligence – https://www.psychologytoday.com/ca/tests/personality/emotional-intelligence-test

Greater Good – https://greatergood.berkeley.edu/quizzes/ei_quiz

HBR – https://hbr.org/2015/06/quiz-yourself-do-you-lead-with-emotional-intelligence

You can also seek professional training, where you will have support materials provided to assess your emotional intelligence and guidance on getting started and staying on track.

Chapter 4

Learning & Developing Emotional Intelligence

To show emotional intelligence (EI), we need to establish a set of inborn qualities that will assist with strengthening our mental well-being daily. The listing below has five ways we can all follow aside from professional EI training to grow in ourselves and be mindful of it.

Negative emotions

Emotional intelligence relies on our ability to identify and manage our emotions. It has to do with how well we can work on our feelings, self-regulate our negative emotions well, build our resiliency and handle stress. If we can identify the feelings that bring us down and understand how we are feeling in a specific moment or situation, we will be less likely to feel overwhelmed by external factors that may drain our mental energy.

So, where do we start? I've listed some of the things I've learned to develop EI within myself:

- When someone says or does something that causes you to be upset, whether using harsh words or offensive jokes, what most people advise in this situation is not to react immediately.

Take a moment, pause, remove yourself from the heat of that moment and take the time to collect your thoughts and choose your response wisely.

- Do not jump to conclusions. Keep your thoughts and feeling in check, so it does not end up clouding your reactions or judgment in the situation.
- When interpersonal conflict or distress is at play, make time to investigate the situation at hand from the other person's perspective. What are the cause and the effects? Try to place yourself in their shoes, understanding what made the other person behave in that way.

You will notice how your attitude changes the moment you start empathizing rationally with their situation. Empathizing does not have to be a win-lose position. Empathy does not mean weakness or agreement; it means arriving at conclusions while allowing for diverse views.

Self-evaluation

While it is a skill to be able to observe and understand others, it is equally essential to watch ourselves. To increase our awareness and to develop emotional intelligence, we need to objectively assess ourselves and peer inside our actions as if we are a fly on the wall. Challenge your thoughts by frequently asking questions like these:

- Is this the right way of thinking?
- What about the words I have used to express myself? How did these words come across to the other person?

- What would have been my reaction if I was the one to be at the receiving end?
- Is there another way, perspective, or an angle that was missed or that would help support looking into the situation differently?
- Am I on the right track?
- Is my family, colleague, friend, etc. happy with me?

Frequent encounters with the self-enhance perception create humility and keep you grounded together, which contributes to building emotional intelligence.

Self-expression

Self-expression is the expression of one's feelings, ideas, or thoughts, whether in art or life, both personally and professionally; it goes hand in hand with emotional intelligence. One cannot do without the other.

Individuals who can identify and express their thoughts in an adequate way and in a socially acceptable manner are considered to be highly emotional intelligent individuals with self-efficacy.

Honing self-expression is how we bring our focus to healthy communication with others. It is the ability to convey our thoughts naturally in an understandable way and to create solutions with good intentions. Being able to express ourselves to communicate with others appropriately about how we feel is a step towards having a more solution-focused base and to becoming a more self-regulated individual.

Stress management

Past studies have shown that people with emotional clarity and awareness are far better at handling stress than others. Whether in the workplace or a highly stressful situation, be it a family or health crisis, stress and burnout cause us to respond poorly. This impacts our emotional capabilities, which as a result, influences how we react.

It is vital to understand that achieving tremendous success professionally doesn't only happen because we are great at our jobs. Success is a byproduct of how we view the world around us, how we handle our emotions, and how self-aware we are with ourselves and with our surroundings.

When we are exposed to stress without having sufficient coping mechanisms and strategies to help us, we open ourselves to a mixed bag of mental health problems.

We should consciously work on simple stress reduction methods using our senses and staying close to nature. I find staying close to nature helps me a lot in calming down and breathing in the fresh air.

Simple stress management techniques can also make a significant difference in dealing with hardships without getting drained. Consider the following:

- Splash cold water on your face after a stressful encounter. The cooling sensation tends to help reduce anxiety and provides a feeling of freshness. Similarly, when you think of a picture that is frozen in time, your mind will capture a pause to take place, and then it restarts new again.
- Avoid caffeine, alcohol, and smoke during hard times. People resort to these substances more during stressful

situations; it is best to avoid such stimulants when you feel anxious.
- Take time off work and schedule a vacation when stress takes a toll on your body and mind. Go away, recharge, energize, spend some quality time with family or catch up with some friends. Time spent well rested will help you regain insights and build your ability to combat stress more effectively.

Making empathy a daily habit

Empathy is the capacity to see anything through someone other than yourself. This understanding comes with practice as you make room for it to become a daily habit. Learning what causes others to act in this fashion requires significant progress to be made in the development of your emotional intelligence.

Lastly, empathy begins within yourself. Random acts of kindness, such as a writing a thank-you note, or offering to help aging parents, friends, or relatives in need, or even having a heart-to-heart conversation with someone is all it takes to practice leading an empathetic life.

The key is to be willing to let your vulnerability be seen. Opening ourselves, whether listening to a colleague without judging them or accepting harsh words from one who may be under stress, can significantly build our social and emotional intelligence connection, thereby strengthening interpersonal bonds.

Self-paced exercise

Exercise #1

The studies of Daniel Goleman illustrated that an emotionally intelligent person can do the following:

- Recognize their own emotions
- Relate to others' emotions
- Actively listen to others
- Actively participate in interpersonal communication and understand the nonverbal cues of behavior
- Control one's thoughts and feelings
- Effectively manage emotions and express them in a socially acceptable way
- Receive criticisms positively and benefit from them
- Forgive, forget, and move on rationally

Exercise #2

How many of the above qualities can you relate to yourself?

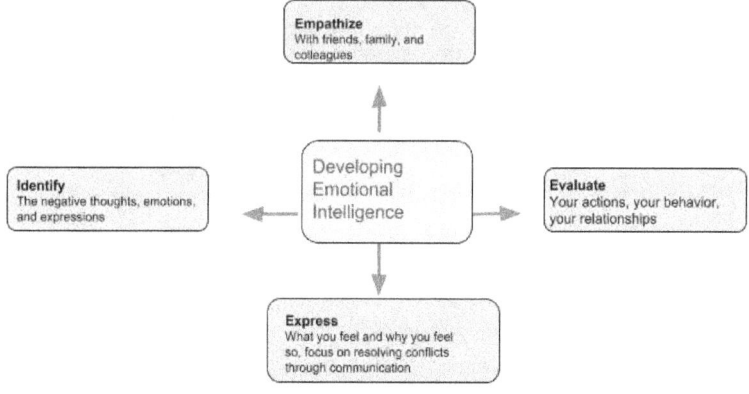

Exercise #3

How many positive and negative emotions can you see? Which are the ones that have affected you the most today? What caused these emotions? You need not to act on them or judge what is right and wrong here. Just focus on observing each feeling and write them down honestly.

Day	Positive Emotions – happy, proud, satisfied, cheerful, enthusiastic, etc.	Why did I feel this?	Negative Emotions – sad, upset, angry, depressed, lonely, insecure, etc.	Why did I feel this?

Mon

Tue

Wed

Thu

Fri

Sat

Sun

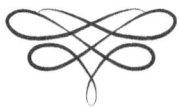

PART 2:

LEADERSHIP THAT MATTERS

Chapter 5

Reflecting On Your Leadership: If It Isn't Broken, Then Break It

Speaking from past experiences, and as one who has moved around within different departments and has worked in various organizations, I seem to stumble upon the same theme every time: What are those traits that may be broken, and what are the ones you need to succeed and move forward? What comes up are these following traits:

Eagerness to improve

Until recently, the cliché was, "If it isn't broken, then don't fix it." Most managers and employees resist change, and they are not so keen on trying to do things differently. Changes cause uneasiness with people in general, whether they are in a power position or not. But in today's ever-changing and fast-evolving business environment, the motto should be, "If it isn't broken, then break it." Employees and managers alike must be willing to re-evaluate and often change how they do things. Being complacent doesn't cut it in a world where almost anything can become obsolete overnight. Occupants of tomorrow's boardrooms will be the executives who aren't afraid to change to improve and stay competitive in their field. So, let's dare to change, dare to be eager, dare to be a better version of ourselves and dare to be different.

Versatility

Organizations look to hire talent based on specific expertise; executives tried to be specialists. A career was built on acquiring a reputation as a systems expert or productivity guru. In today's streamlined corporate world, versatility has become a prized commodity. Thin management ranks are expected to deal competently with unexpected changes in markets, finance, and technology.

Tomorrow's top talents will begin now to gather experience in a wide range of positions. So, why not volunteer for work outside your immediate area? Ask to participate in cross-functional teams; join a committee, or a board, and take time after regular hours to learn new skills.

Interpersonal skills

Executives who can't deal with people confidently and expertly are doomed to failure. You must know how to develop talented staff, motivate employees, communicate instructions, and work with a variety of people. Managers who lack people skills are ill-suited to work in the growing number of "horizontal" organizations—those built around processes rather than functions. These organizations often ask executives to collaborate with peers over whom they have no direct authority. In those situations, an executive's power rests with his/her ability to negotiate directions with no command-and-control structure.

Vision

In the business world, vision is simply a forward outlook of what needs to be done so that the company can anticipate customers' needs. The best managers demonstrate vision by taking the initiative in helping the company meet its goals. When a suggestion is made, they judge it not only on its immediate merits but on whether it will move the company closer to its strategic goals. Before any action, they measure possible consequences and whether it makes strategic sense for the company.

Empathy

In today's business world, your employees are your most significant assets, so treat them well. Loyal employees result in loyal customers. What's that got to do with empathy? It's simple: you can't lead without empathy, and you can't succeed without empathy. People want to follow someone they can trust, believe in and share values with. Empathy is the cornerstone to creating and developing connections with your customers, clients, and colleagues. Now more than ever, to impact long-lasting positive change, there is a call to all business leaders to lead with empathy. It's the birthmark of vulnerability and kindness. That's where all the magic of transformation takes place if we allow it into the corporate world.

Many executives don't recognize what skills they lack. Ask friends or trusted colleagues about how you're doing. Once you identify deficiencies, take immediate steps to overcome them. No one has it all; if that were the case, we'd be living in a perfect world, and there would be no need for improvement or growth.

Self-paced exercise

Take some time out now to do a bit of self-reflection and look inward to answer the following questions.

- What are your top three strengths that you practice the most as a leader?
- What are your bottom three strengths that you haven't been able to practice?
- What is your leadership vision?
- Who do you want to become when you are the best version of yourself?
- What is your leadership philosophy?
- What kind of a leader do you need to become?
- What do you need to adjust to create the impact that you want to see?
- What do you need to change in yourself and leave behind?
- If you were one of your team members that were led by your current self, would you be satisfied?
- If we ask your future self about the lessons that are learned, what would your future self-tell you?
- What are you noticing as you answer these questions?
- With this new awareness, what are you willing to do differently as of today?
- Have I made it crystal clear what is expected of the individual/team?
- Have I shared my goals and challenges? Do I share the big picture?
- Have I ensured adequate resources are in place?
- Have I cultivated a learning environment where curiosity and sharing are encouraged?

- Have I provided timely and constructive feedback regularly?
- Have I secured the most appropriate training and coaching for the required skills?
- Have I created a safe environment to fail, to learn, to grow?
- Have I checked in to see what motivates others?
- Have I sought regular feedback for myself and other senior leaders?
- Do my actions line up with my words? Am I walking the talk?
- Is my finger always pointed outward, or do I take responsibility for the situation?
- Do I make time for my people? Am I accessible and present when they need me?
- Do I facilitate development through meaningful dialogue, coaching, and support?

Source: Talyaa Varder and Catherine Harrison

Chapter 6

Leadership – What Gets In The Way Of Building An Engaged Team?

In teams and organizations, heart, emotion, and especially vulnerability are both liabilities and weaknesses. These traits/qualities are considered more human than business behaviors. Simply put, some may say they don't belong in a professional business setting at all. Most people will say, who has the time to deal with that? Or they are not trained in handling those situations. Perhaps if we open ourselves "to be truly seen," then we risk ourselves being exposed, shamed, judged misunderstood or viewed as weak.

After all, what we've been taught over the years is to understand certain aspects of workplace authority. Leadership qualities, perceptions, traits, or characteristics are about strength, knowledge, power, status, excellence, etc. However, many articles, studies, and business blogs have written about leadership, providing a clear perspective on what authentic leadership means. For this chapter, I will touch on what open leadership looks like versus closed-minded leadership.

But before I do, I want talk about what gets in the way of leaders daring to lead. Maybe it's because of culture, or in some cases, individual leaders are too comfortable and driven by their egos, so they lock up the heart and seal it off from feelings. They praise and reward perfectionism, emotional hardness, and the false compartmentalizing of our lives and work. They keep things easy, comfortable, and less messy instead of embracing the tough and awkward conversations. They value "all knowing" over always learning and staying curious.

Starting with *perfectionism,* this is a self-destructive and addictive belief and an unattainable goal. It's a clear pathway to feelings of shame, judgment, and blame. Its consequence is fostering fear and failure. It fuels the primary thoughts of "Everything needs to be perfect" or "What will people think?"

You end up putting yourself through the path of "please, perform, perfect, and prove." You dangerously adopt a debilitating belief system that says, "I am what I accomplish and how well I accomplish it." Having honest and open conversations about perfectionism within trusting and brave teams can be healing and powerful. Asking questions on how perfectionism shows up, and how you can distinguish perfectionism from striving for excellence in a healthy way. Are there ways to check in with each other that works for everyone? Are there flags, warning signs, or indicators that everyone can take accountability for spotting? If there is space and willingness within a trusted environment, it will result in profound changes: the teams will grow closer, performance will increase, and trust will be built in the process.

Scarcity and foreboding

When something great happens in your life, or let's say you get promoted at work, or you delivered high sales results, how many times do you celebrate only to find yourself thinking,

"Don't get so happy or comfortable; it's not over yet." Your thoughts are inviting disaster or waiting for the shoe to drop. Joy is a vulnerable emotion. When we feel joy, it's felt from a place of beauty and fragility and deep gratitude from a state or fact of lasting only for a limited period, all combined in one experience.

When you can't tolerate that level of vulnerability, joy becomes foreboding (as the author Brené Brown describes in her book *Dare to lead*). The feelings of disappointment or pictures of hurt wash over us and take our thoughts and minds hostage, robbing us from the joyful moments we experience with our successes and accomplishments.

How does foreboding joy show up at work? Usually, not in obvious ways, so it's hard to recognize at times when it's happening. Sometimes, we are hesitant to celebrate victories because we are either afraid that if we celebrate with our team or breathe, something might go wrong. For example, when you start a project or roll out a new system, you don't want to celebrate yet because you are not sure if it's going to work.

We also withhold recognition because we don't want employees to get too excited; there's still more work to be done, so we don't want them to get complacent or too relaxed, and we don't want to set a precedent. Most times, biased leaders tend to do the opposite of everything by going overboard when it's unnecessarily called for.

Lack of empathy

One of the most important qualities a leader should have is empathy. How many of us have gone through a very profound or difficult situation in life that impacted our work or level of engagement? How do leaders handle situations when a member of their team is going through a difficult time? That determines the kind of leader you are. Do you show up for the members of your team? Do you extend empathy and kindness toward your employees when they need it most?

Empathy builds on connection and trust. It's an essential ingredient for teams who take risks and show up. Our job is to connect; it's not our job to make things better. Empathy is connecting to the feeling under the experience, not to the experience itself. If you ever felt grief, disappointment, shame, fear, loneliness, or anger, you are qualified. Now you need the courage to practice and build your empathy skills. If someone is sharing something difficult, your truthful response to not knowing what to say is better than trying to find a "response" to say. The connection is what heals.

Empathy is a choice, and this choice is a vulnerable one. For me to connect with you through empathy would mean I would have to connect with something in myself that shares that same feeling or emotion. In the face of a difficult conversation, when we see that someone's hurt or in pain, it's our instinct as human beings to try to make it better or fix it.

We give advice, but empathy isn't about fixing. It's the brave choice to be with someone in their darkness, not to race to turn on the light so we feel better. Empathy has the ability to see the world as others see it, to take their perspective, to be nonjudgmental, to understand another person's feelings, and to communicate your understanding of that person's feelings. It's being mindful and taking a balanced approach to negative emotions so that feelings are neither suppressed nor exaggerated. That way, we cannot ignore our pain and feel compassion for it.

Fitting-in culture

In her book *Braving the Wilderness,* Brené Brown shares this definition of true belonging:

"True belonging is the spiritual practice of believing in and belonging to yourself so deeply that you can share your most authentic self with the world and find sacredness in both being part of something and standing alone in the wilderness. True belonging doesn't require you to change who you are; it requires you to be who are."

When leaders and companies miss the mark on their culture, the barrier to true belonging is fitting in or changing who we are so we can be accepted. When we create a culture of fitting in, and of seeking approval and likeability at work, we are not only stifling individuality; we are limiting people's sense of true belonging.

People desperately want to be part of something bigger than themselves, and they want to experience a profound connection with others. Still, they don't want to sacrifice their authenticity, freedom, or power to do it. Only when a diverse perspective is included, respected and valued can we start to get the full picture of the world, who we are, how we serve, what the needs are and how successfully we meet people where they are.

Seeing worthiness through productivity

We are at a time of cultural crisis pertaining to busyness and sleep deprivation. As a society, we still struggle with equating our self-worth to our net worth. When self-worth is seen as a measure of productivity, we inevitably lose the ability to slow down or stop. The idea of doing something that doesn't add to the bottom line provokes stress and anxiety. We convince ourselves that downtime is a waste of precious time when we can work and get things done.

If we want to live a life of meaning and contribution, we must become intentional about cultivating sleep and play. We must let go of exhaustion, busyness, and productivity as status symbols and measures of self-worth. We impress no one! Leaders need to model appropriate boundaries by shutting off emails at a reasonable time and focusing on themselves and their families.

Do not celebrate people who work through the weekend or those who brag that they were tethered to their laptops over the holiday break. Ultimately, it's an unsustainable behavior, and it has dangerous side effects, including burnout, depression, and anxiety. It also creates a culture of workaholic competitiveness that's detrimental to everyone.

Now let's shift to what it looks like to lead from a close-minded leadership style versus leading from a place of openness. This was extracted from Brené Brown's book Dare to Lead.

Closed-minded leadership style:
- Using power over
- Numbing
- Driving perfectionism and fostering fear of failure
- Tolerating discrimination, echo chambers, and a "fitting in" culture
- Collecting gold stars
- Zigzagging and avoiding

- Leading from hurt and insecurity
- Hustling for self-worth
- The victim or Viking: crush or be crushed
- Fear and uncertainty
- Being a knower and being right
- "This is how it's going to be done" mentality

Open-minded leadership style:

- Modeling and encouraging healthy striving, empathy, and self-compassion
- Practicing gratitude and celebrating milestones and victories
- Being a learner and getting it right
- Modeling clarity, kindness, and hope
- Knowing values
- Cultivating commitment and a shared purpose
- Cultivating a culture of belonging, inclusivity, and diverse perspectives and acceptance
- Giving gold stars
- Straight talking and taking action
- Leading from the heart
- Acknowledging, naming and normalizing collective fear and uncertainty
- Transparency

- Setting boundaries and finding real comfort
- Using power with, power to and power within

Self-paced exercise

Here are some signs of what an engaged team is supposed to look like (Olivia Curtis, Wellness Specialist, CPT, FNS):

- Goes above and beyond and steps up to help their coworkers ("I've got your back" mentality)
- Uplifting and positive in their conversations
- Dedicated to the company
- Higher effort and quality of work
- A proactive approach
- Open mindset
- Low turnarounds of employees
- Promotion from within
- Glassdoor reviews and employee surveys that reflect excellent ratings and comments
- The bottom line is growing
- Collaboration is a cornerstone of the organization and built into the company's values
- Open and adaptive to change (agile)
- Implements changes quickly
- Passionate about their work

- Accountability and trust are their language and in the DNA of their work
- Take pride in their personal and professional development
- Social engagement
- Smiles often
- Approachable
- Positive culture/environment
- The team is full of brilliant ideas
- Easy to recruit and keep top talents
- Self-starters who believe their success is mutually dependent on the success of their team and company
- Proud brand ambassadors of the company
- Knowledge sharing

Chapter 7

Leadership: Team Management – Turn An Ordinary Team Into A Hot Team

There is no shortage of creativity when businesses get creative with icebreakers and fun team-building exercises for team management. This includes everything from scavenger hunts, community walks, or runs to building with Legos. While you are spending time working on new ways to pump up your teams, the question that comes up is, how do you take this ordinary team and turn it into a hot team? Management consultant Laurence Haughton offers this advice for turning ordinary groups into hot teams:

- Don't become rule bound. Rules are generally intended to streamline and safeguard work. They can also hamstring your operation when common sense calls for exceptions. Don't be so rigid, annually reviewing tasks and business operations.

- Don't criticize in public. Never embarrass employees in front of the team. Actions like that will only come back to bite you. Managers like that think they're holding people accountable, but they are wrong. What they're doing is fueling payback.

- Show you care. If you genuinely like your people, show them. They will enjoy helping you when it's crunch time.

- Listen, both in one-on-ones and in groups. Listening takes practice. It helps you correct any misinformation, and it relaxes barriers, increases trust, and lets people feel good knowing what they do for a living makes a difference.

- Make it their mission. Even when a task or project is less than exciting, you can still make the work more engaging. Creating and delegating roles for each person, for example, gives people a sense of being special.

- Let them decide. Allowing people to control their processes boosts morale. Just make sure those processes keep improving.

Bring the energy from the off-site team-building experience back to the office

Typically, off-site meetings are saddled with PowerPoint presentations, flip charts, and a couple of team-building exercises. But back at work months later, what changes? Take the time to find an off-site event that leaves your team not only energized and focused but also able to bring that energy to the workspace.

Know what victory looks like

How will you know if you've achieved victory? If you need to revamp and add new products, then hold an off-site event to jump-start things. Invite designers, engineers, and marketers from the company to spend one week hashing it out. A process that generally takes years will result in meeting goals. Having a concrete goal defines the line between exploring creative flights of fancy and remaining results driven.

Make sure your team-building exercises can relate to solving a real-world problem and not something that is done for fun. Fun and drinking festivities will always have a time and place, so don't forget to plan for those as well.

During one of the Ford company's off-site events, Carolyn Lantz, the executive director of brand imaging, gave the executives $50 each, and off they went on a bus to an Old Navy store. "I instructed them, 'You have 20 minutes to find and purchase an outfit that you must wear in the morning tomorrow. You are busy people who look for great design at a great price. Those are our (Ford's) customers.'" The exercise was completed to make a point: Ford's products need to be well designed, but democratically priced. (Adapted from "Can This Off-Site Be Saved?" Cheryl Dahle, Fast Company, www.FastCompany.com)

Team complacency

Soon after a team forms, the excitement often peaks. Teammates dream of big accomplishments, they set big goals, and each will commit to collaboration.

But often, when the initial enthusiasm begins to wane, the "spirited atmosphere" fades, and a more static routine sets in. The senior executives who attended the first few team meetings begin to call in absent. New developments (or urgent crises!) within the business now redirect management's focus away from the group's activities. Some of the team members start slacking off or immersing themselves in other projects. This invariably leaves less time for them to devote to the group as well.

If you begin to see this pattern unfold at your workplace, it's time to step in and breathe new life into your team. Five strategies may help here:

Inject new blood: Begin by inviting a few high-energy types to join the team. Don't put them in charge. They would threaten the team leader, and the informal hierarchy that's already formed should be maintained. Instead, ask them to lend their talents and revitalize the group.

Tape the team: Do this when you want to jolt a team to rise to a higher level. Lecturing a team to improve will often fall upon deaf ears. Making a video of their recent meetings can show just how listless the meetings have become.

Turn your team into trainers: Maybe the solution is to form a new team. Ask your current group to serve as an "advisory board" to it. Arrange for the tenured to coach the newbies. Encourage them to share their experiences regarding teamwork and the process to get there. Identify and isolate the kind of behaviors that create better collaboration. Creating a buddy system might be a good thing, whereby each of the "seasoned team members" mentors a team member in the new group.

Strip away routine: Study and identify how a tired team got to this point. Add disruption to the mix by having the group meet in new places (a client's facility, your home) and find new ways to work together. Instead of the team breaking into the same small cliques, juggle the group so individuals who typically don't work closely together will have an opportunity to get to know each other better. Perhaps it may be time to rearrange the seating configuration so everyone's in a circle facing each other.

Host an outing: Try inviting the team to join you on a weekend hike or family picnic, or on scheduled fun activities (cooking classes, escape room, chocolate making, etc.). This is an excellent time for participants to get to know each other with their guard down. Even if you already tried this early on, do it again now that the team has been together for a while. When the group returns to work, they'll have a newfound camaraderie, which will translate into more trust and better teamwork.

Self-paced exercise

Below are a few suggestions to try out with your team(s). Hopefully one of them will help spur the team on to achieve the creativity or closeness intended in order to make it a memorable experience!

- Scavenger Hunt
- What's My Name?
- Cook-Off
- Sneak a Peek
- Board Game Tournament
- Office Trivia
- Improv Workshop
- Two Truths and a Lie
- Karaoke Night
- Go-Kart Racing

- Professional Development Workshop
- Jigsaw Puzzle Race
- Room Escape Games
- The Egg Drop Challenge
- Laser Tag
- Catch Phrase
- Volunteer
- Mystery Dinner
- Kayaking/Canoeing
- Memory Wall
- Painting Class
- Cooking Class
- Explore a New Place
- Sports Game
- Potluck, Bowling

Chapter 8

Tips For Managers On Trusting Employees

Wouldn't it be easy if there was a handy manual that everyone could refer to for building trust and sustaining trusting relationships, etc.?

Unfortunately, only when one loses trust do they realize how important and valuable trust it. So, in organizations, how can managers foster a culture that is built on trust? We have all seen missions and value statements that are set by different organizations. Those are the guiding principles and the glue of what a company represents, stands for, and values. But the real question is, how can employees and organizations demonstrate those values daily? It starts with the executives and managers from the top-down, leading by example: how they conduct themselves in meetings and during their performance appraisal discussions with their direct reports.

Putting it all together to bring the best outcome and reactions from people in general, one must understand that deep down, we all strive for love and belonging, to be recognized, to be valued for our contributions, to have equal opportunities, and to be understood and appreciated. When there are issues, you must put biased opinions and external noises aside; you must remain neutral and look to solve the issue instead of wasting time on the blame. There are steps to consider that can be a starting point as you build trust foundations among your employees or team members on developing and maintaining trust, such as…

Lead by example

- Do what you say you'll do
- Accept accountability
- Be scrupulous about confidentiality
- Encourage a culture of continuous improvement
- Avoid creating a culture of blame

Show that you care about others

- Spend time with people
- Show your appreciation
- Be available
- Support employees
- Celebrate successes and milestones

Empower your employees

- Trust people to make the right decisions
- Make yourself available as a coach
- Focus on goals
- Look for ways to help employees grow
- Play to people's strengths

Encourage open communication

- Commit to being open and honest
- Share what you know with employees

- Create an open-door work environment
- Encourage employees to ask questions and to offer suggestions

Treat everyone fairly and with respect

- Avoid favoritism
- Create a working environment that's free of discrimination, harassment, intimidation and bullying
- Look for the good in all your employees

Building trust doesn't happen overnight. It grows over time from your consistent actions and words.

> An employee's motivation is a direct result of the sum of interactions with his or her manager.
>
> Bob Nelson

PART 3:

LEARNING & IMPROVING YOURSELF

Chapter 9

Why A Mentoring Connection Is So Important?

Mentoring isn't new. Now more than ever, it is an essential career tool for managers. People have different views and theories about mentoring. Some think of it to advance their careers. Once the goal of career advancement has been accomplished, you move on and outgrow it.

Others think of it as having an advisor or a cheerleader by their side celebrating their wins, advising them on risks, guiding them towards their goals and helping them strategically to advance and develop at every stage of their career.

Career paths are becoming more complicated as you reach toward the upper rungs of the corporate ladder, and there are benefits both to having a mentor or being one. Some companies understand the importance of mentoring, and several of them have established formal mentoring programs, which can take many forms.

In some organizations, potential prospects are assigned a mentor, so they don't have to go through the haphazard, often unlucky, process of trying to find one on their own.

At other companies, the practice is more extensive. For example, they install a program that assigns every employee a "peer advisor." Or they have a "mentor-up" program, a reverse mentoring system in which managers are assigned a female mentor one to two reporting levels below them to foster "positive relationships" between bosses of either sex to help build awareness of issues facing women.

Why mentoring is so important: formal or informal

Mentoring is more prevalent today for several reasons:

- A mentor can provide protection from corporate upheavals. In an uncertain corporate environment, which has become the "normal" way of describing today's corporate world, mentoring can provide a safe harbor while you develop in your position.

- A mentor can act as a cross-cultural bridge in global corporations. For example, as growing numbers of global companies operate in Canada and the United States, the mentor can facilitate learning customs, rules, and protocols, benefiting both the mentor and the mentee.

- The mentee can provide his mentor with valuable information from below; it works both ways. At the same time, the mentor can open important political doors for him/her.

- Mentoring can help people rise through the ranks. It is especially useful for women, who traditionally have lacked role models and champions in the executive suite. A woman who aligns herself with a male/female higher up in the organization can learn valuable lessons and have an important ally on her climb to the top.

Get yourself picked: How do you find a mentor if your company doesn't have a program?

The magic word is visibility, which can be accomplished in the following ways:

1. Get assigned to projects in which you can contribute your talents.

2. When you write reports or presentations, hand-deliver your completed work instead of sending it. Constant interaction is vital for establishing a comfortable rapport with a potential mentor.

3. Ask questions. This is an excellent way to make yourself known and to share your ideas and opinions.

4. Consider everyone as a potential mentor. Look at every person in the company; keep your eyes and ears open when you meet people. When you find someone, you think you can learn from, approach them directly, and ask if they can be your mentor.

5. Look outside your network/company. Join professional groups in your field and function. Also, for women, join a women's organization and seek a mentor there.

6. Think about where you need help. For example, if you are heavy on organizational skills but weak on financials, seek a mentor who can help you learn to read a corporate balance sheet better.

7. Find a good fit. It has to be someone you feel safe with, someone you trust, someone you feel believes in you and is enthusiastic about you. This is essential for the success

of the mentorship. Also, your mentor should be open to learning from you, as well.

Drawbacks to mentoring

The mentor you find may not be the best teacher for you or may fall out of favor with senior management, taking you out too. Here are suggestions for avoiding these traps:

- When looking for a mentor, be sure you know what you want from the relationship. Hold prospective mentors up to specific criteria and ask them about their criteria. What do they hope to gain from the relationship in terms of work and political goals? How strong are their alliances?

- Are they good teachers and motivators? Some mentors will oversee your career but do little to enhance your knowledge of the job. At some point, you will have to stand by yourself.

- Would you pose a threat to your mentor? Some people are very good when they're mentoring several levels down in the organization, but when a mentee begins to draw even, new rules come into play. To avoid problems in the future, try to find out how your mentor treated previous mentees or if they ever mentored anyone before.

Managing the mentor

Never burn any bridges between you and the rest of the organization. Don't assume you're forever protected by your mentor or part of that person's group. No matter how good your relationship with your mentor, do not develop a false sense of security. During the mentoring relationship, ask yourself if your goals are being met. If not, why not?

- Maintain your alliances. Avoid dissension and establish good relationships with everyone, dodge political hassles.
- If your situation does not improve after the first year of mentoring, consider finding a new mentor. You can accomplish this diplomatically by gradually easing into a new relationship while loosening your ties with your former mentor.

The importance of being a mentor

Don't overlook the advantages of being a mentor to someone else in your organization. That's the best part. You can use it to rise through the ranks yourself. As you mentor someone, you will have increased confidence and feel a sense of fulfillment, and your self-esteem will naturally rise. You will shine more, and your bosses will notice. Plus, you'll be mastering your people skills, and that's a critical criterion when you are evaluated for promotion. Finally, you can't help but gain experience, as the teacher always learns from his students.

Chapter 10

Overcoming Obstacles To Success

There are many obstacles to overcome to be successful. This is given no matter what endeavor you are pursuing. The reality is such that there are going to be issues, and roadblocks along the way are guaranteed. After all, we all know success is not easy, and the journey to achieve our success stories, whether professionally or personally, has its peaks and valleys; you have to be ready for it. Below are listed a few suggestions that might help to manage them when they happen:

Root cause troubleshooting and diagnosis

Find the root cause first, and you've just found the quickest way of solving a problem. It will take some time to determine. However, it will be time well spent because once you know the root cause, you know what you are dealing with so you can address it and move on.

Research the problem online

The internet is a massive archive of ideas for solving almost any problem. If you run into an obstacle or barrier, someone else most likely has as well. Use the internet's collective wisdom to help you develop a plan.

Get assistance from others

Recruit your co-workers, family, or friends to help you think of ways to overcome the obstacle. Different people will each have different perspectives on the situation that can often lead to a breakthrough. Sometimes the solutions are right there in places where you least expect them. When we are too consumed focusing on the obstacle, we get into stockiness mode versus troubleshooting.

Ask an expert

If the problem is in an area that is outside your expertise, you might find it useful to bring in an expert. It could be a coach, a counselor, etc., but make sure he/she has solved similar challenges in the past. Change your attitude toward the situation, evaluate your approach, and see if there is a change in the way you are looking at the situation that might help to overcome the obstacle. Sometimes, the problem starts with "us."

Using trial and error

Experimenting will be needed if all else fails or when your situation is unique. Progress slowly while evaluating each of your solutions as carefully as possible. You may find that it takes a combination of solutions to achieve the best results. Don't be afraid or regret the trial-and-error process. I have come to learn they have been the best guide to most of the success and accomplishment I have achieved professionally and personally. It's within the uncomfortable space of the trial and errors that I have experienced the most growth and wisdom.

Sleep on it

Sometimes, our brains require time to rest before getting back to work on the issue. So, if you feel you don't want to deal at the moment, then it's best to take some time to sleep on it. Once you are ready to pick up where you left off, the reality is the obstacle, or the problem is not going anywhere. So, you might as well be in the right frame of mind when you need to deal with it.

Never give up

Perseverance is what will lead to success. Persist until you find a solution, no matter what the odds are against you. Resiliency is vital in helping you to get back up every time and bounce back.

Starting fresh

When all else fails, start again at the beginning. Re-evaluate everything. Maybe one of the assumptions you've had about a specific obstacle is wrong. It is likely that because you are having a hard time, you haven't identified the root cause yet or have not framed the issue you are having correctly.

Problematic behavioral thought patterns

Barriers commonly take the form of attitudes, behavior patterns, rigid beliefs, fears, and real or imagined deficiencies in your skills that somehow impede your progress. While it's not possible to eliminate all these barriers, it is possible to manage them or move ahead despite them. By admitting the existence of the hampering characteristic or attitude and observing how and when it shows up as a block, you can begin to modify the effects of any negative trait.

Acknowledging the barriers is step number one. Recognize that everyone has barriers or attitude impediments and that only those who are willing to work can deal with them effectively or eliminate them. Internal walls can be reflective of your style characteristics. Therefore, compare your internal barriers with your style and career type. Try to identify whether individual attitudes stem from your work type or if they can accurately be termed personal deficiencies you want to overcome.

Internal barriers

You may wonder what some of these internal barriers and personality characteristics are that may give you difficulty on the job or outside of work. You may say, "I tend to *be* or *have*" the following:

- A showoff
- A workaholic
- Absentminded
- Abrupt
- Autocratic
- Black-or-white thinking
- Bossy and dominating
- Bitter
- Burnt-out
- Aloof

- All-or-nothing behavior
- Distrustful of others
- Cynical
- Easily hurt feelings
- Fear of change or fear of making mistakes
- Hard-headed
- Disorganized
- Feelings of inadequacy
- Moody
- Limited attention span
- Self-doubt
- Skeptical

Final thoughts

It's an endless list, and I believe you know where I am going with this. The idea is that you select a handful of work-related internal barriers that you would most like to reduce or eliminate from your work or life. Choose five essential work-related internal barriers currently in need of reduction or elimination. You will find over time that almost every goal you chase will have its walls in your way. For you to succeed, you need to master the art of problem-solving. Move past the hurdles as quickly as you can to cross the finish line!

Chapter 11

Transparency – Don't Make It Personal, And You Will Thrive!

Quite some time ago, I had an assignment working for an executive that spoke a lot about *transparency* among teams and employees. In this chapter, I will summarize my observations, learnings, and takeaways on the topic of transparency.

Observations– Whenever the executive spoke, whether in meetings, events, etc., employees were completely in tune. He was very articulate, always had the buy-in of the group, and commanded any room, allowing him the opportunity to speak. It was great to listen to and learn from him. Everyone in the room listened with admiration (dare I say adoration?) to this executive. He was always on the list to be invited to all sorts of engagement and events. Boy, he had nailed the motivation and transparency talk down to a T. He was willing to confront subjects where no other executives within the organization were ready to tackle. He would take on topics such as honesty, the glass ceiling, diversity, teamwork, cultures, and challenging the status quo. Everyone who knew him was inspired by him and wanted to take a page from his book.

As time passes, like most organizations, changes in leadership roles (a.k.a. re-org) will happen. For this executive, the changes within the organization impacted his career goals, as he was not moved forward on the previous two occasions.

With the changes delaying his progression, his message of "transparency" talks had begun to follow his mood and changed over time as well. Transparency in his books now changed from open and upfront to delivering only certain information and doing so when and if it suited his agenda and goals.

Example #1: He said to all teams that everyone could grow in the company. He spoke of his plans to grow as well. Once his career path slowed significantly, his tone changed to advising the teams to "suck it up, grow in your current roles and be proud of where you are."

Example #2: He spoke to team members regarding promotion opportunities and that he was always available for open and honest dialogue. In reality, openings were filled from outside the departments along with no notification to the current team so they could apply.

When you're transparent, you reveal that you have nothing to hide. This, in turn, invites trust from your peers, and so forth. Basically, in the eyes of others, your "brand" is that of an honest, credible person. It is not without its challenges, though, as the prospect of being open and vulnerable may make you nervous at times. For some, the digital world has made observing transparency an inescapable option.

Learnings – What I've learned about transparency is that it's about always being honest irrespective of the planned outcome. It is not when it suits the situation. If you are going to use it when it suits your agenda, over time, people will take notice. As such, the pulling and hiding of transparency cards do not help one's brand in the long run. It may also affect your corporate brand if left unchecked. Specifically, if all along that's what you have been selling people on, it will uncover itself when confronted by reality.

Transparency is about understanding what's at stake and being able to speak the truth, no matter what the outcome is. Unless you are ready to be brave, step out courageously, and be seen in the arena with your employees, team members, friends, and people in general, you can't use it on a part-time basis or on your terms. It's either that you are fully transparent, or you are not! Don't advertise it if you can't always use it consistently. Your brand integrity will suffer; you will lose your followers and believers; you will become nothing other than someone who lives a life of double standards. These morals only suit themselves rather than for the greater good.

Takeaways – My takeaways from an observational standpoint, and of having the fortune of sitting on both sides of the leadership table gathering some thoughts, are listed below:

What transparency is to me:

- Honesty, being absolutely honest, and more honest without limitations; the facts will help, not hinder, the course for open dialogue

- Tangible actions that are followed by inspired words, commitments, and promises

- Speaking the truth free of judgment, criticisms, deceits, or manipulations

- Intent is pure

- Willingness to have uncomfortable and difficult conversations in order to grow personally and professionally
- It is courage, so there is no room for fear
- To believe or stand for something when no one else does
- Change for the greater good
- To lead by example always
- To understand what is at stake and to choose to do the right thing
- To make room for what is acceptable and equal
- To educate, teach and inspire in all facets of life
- It is humility at its best
- Consistent words followed by one's actions, values, and moral beliefs
- To make room for vulnerability when no one wants to
- It is confidence for breaking free
- It is challenging the status quo
- It is a long-life process to live by

What transparency is not to me?

- Enlarged and inflated egos
- Put-downs or teardowns of people
- Convenient for when/how/who/and what
- It is not part-time use

- It is not just using inspiring words, optimized to attract followers
- Does not allow room for lies, manipulations or deceits
- It is not a betrayal
- Something that makes you flip flop sides to save yourself
- Selfish
- It is not situational; either you are fully in or fully out
- A false brand – it is your "brand," so if using it, use it wisely and carefully
- It is not to be used cloaked as diplomacy; it will always create an unstable foundation this way
- It is not made up stories to sell as realities and truth

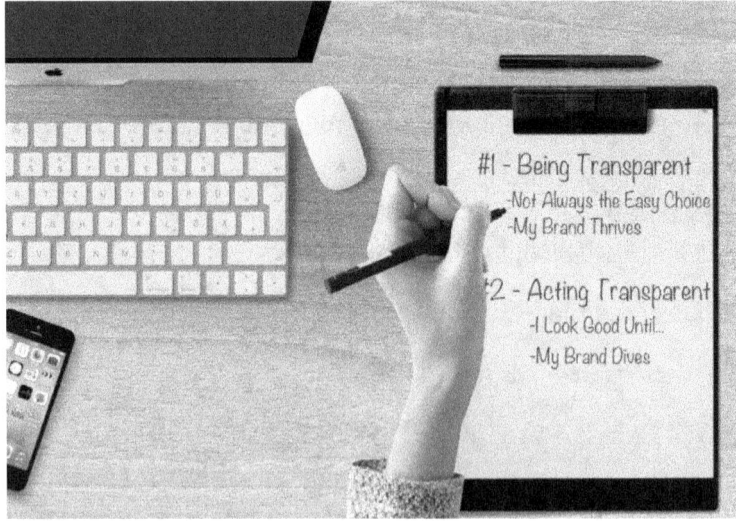

If you are going to use *transparency* as your brand, you must be careful as to how your interpretation of transparency compares to what it means to the majority. In the workplace, we tend to face some realities and situations that will alter our views, as we continue to climb the corporate ladder in our quest to attain the highest level of success professionally. For some, though, they are unable to see the chaos and debris left behind in their pursuit of higher accomplishments and excellence.

Therefore, either you are fully transparent, or you are not. But you can't be both! So, chose one and stick with it. At least that way, you don't have to worry about your brand image or continuing to conduct damage control in the long run.

Chapter 12

Employee Evaluation: Measuring Intangible Traits

It's the same thing every year. Supervisors sit with their teams individually and follow the standardized performance review process. This format is one that tends to avoid or, at best, "dip a toe" in the waters of critical intangible factors such as cooperativeness, dependability, and judgment. It is important to note, though, that the higher up the organizational chart, the greater the importance these intangible traits become.

Unsurprisingly, the majority of supervisors find these intangibles the most difficult traits (factors) to evaluate on paper. It may be because these appear on the surface to be deeply personal. It is much easier to remain objective on an evaluation of hitting measured, tangible goals. It is a bit harder to base an individual's achievement solely on their personality or human merit. Though intangible factors may seem personal, they are critical to effectively maintaining positive working relationships and hitting the tangible targets.

To assess an employee's intangibles, you first need to identify which traits are vital for the role. Cooperativeness might be critical for an individual working on a team project, for example. Identifying initiative would be ideal for creative types of building or designing websites, marketing campaigns, or business development.

Before your review with an employee, take time to identify the intangible factors included in the individual's performance standards. If done correctly, you should have no issue answering to yourself why the employee has rated the score they will be receiving. This will help to draw a tangible score (measurement) to an intangible trait.

The following questions will assist in measuring the intangibles related to each category listed.

Planning
1. Does the employee set measurable short- and long-term goals?
2. Are the employee's goals in tune with company needs?
3. Does the employee's planning show sound assumptions that reflect the company's goals, objectives, and resources?
4. Does the employee typically achieve the expected results and deliver them promptly?

Organization
1. Is the employee aware of what is going on in his or her department, including who is doing what?
2. Does the employee know what the department can do in an emergency?
3. Does the employee do an excellent job of delegating work according to subordinates' abilities?

Intelligence
1. Does the employee see relationships between facts and draw appropriate conclusions quickly?
2. Does the employee learn from the experience?

Judgment

1. When confronted with an emergency, does the employee quickly recognize the most critical priorities?
2. Does the employee think through the financial implications of his or her decisions?
3. Does he or she make decisions quickly, but not hastily?

Initiative

1. Does the employee anticipate what must be done?
2. Does the employee perform well in the absence of superiors?
3. Has the employee made original suggestions to improve operations?

Leadership

1. Does the employee explain rather than command?
2. Do people listen closely when he or she speaks?
3. Does the employee spell out the benefits of doing things his or her way?
4. Does he or she deal smoothly with unexpected developments?

It's hard not to be subjective when evaluating intangible factors; we are human after all. An excellent way to avoid subjective influence is to focus on concrete examples of times (instances) that the employee has displayed respectively to a particular trait, both positive and negative.

Documentation is your most critical historical guide. Keep simple performance logs/notes for each employee, which can also be integrated into the 1:1 meeting. These meetings give a unique perspective on an employee's strengths and challenges affecting positive and negative behavior.

Keep your notes current. When the time comes to discuss intangibles with your employee during a feedback session or in a formal setting, tie the traits to tangible examples of workplace wins and losses. As an example, you may praise an employee for extra efforts to resolve an issue. Perhaps bring in help or an ad-hoc team to restore business productivity.

Help your employees reach and maintain their peak performance by defining what high performance is. Share this expectation and vision of what high performance looks like to you. It is also important to show how to get to that high-performance target.

This is best achieved by involving your employees in setting goals. Keep these goals realistic being aware that employees will have their motivations. Find out what the motives are to help meet consensus to achieve a favorable acceptance. Once this is complete, get out of the way and avoid micro-managing. They now have the tools, goals, and resources.

Enough cannot be stated about trust in the workplace. It is shown to inspire your employees to do their jobs by going the extra mile. Trust creates healthy spaces between employees and managers. Trust leads to a culture of empowerment and allows for valued contributions to the business objectives. Practiced collectively, this leads to success, and a "win-win" environment with collaboration and respect entrenched within the company culture.

Other intangible traits that sets you apart from everyone else:
- **Grit:** the ability, the drive, and passion to keep going, to get up after you fail, and to try and try again. It's the unfailing effort and energy you put into everything you

do repeatedly. It's when you expect something is challenging to be done, but you believe you still can do it.

- **Self-awareness:** You understand that your history, experience, and upbringing have brought you to the place that you are today. Each person understands their world because of the story they've grown up in. Self-reflection helps us understand when we are doing something wrong or why we are driven to do it.

- **Resourcefulness:** This is the ability to problem-solve your way out of a situation. It's a way to look at things differently or to come up with solutions that might not be readily available. It's the ability to learn with what you've got or to find new ways to do things.

- **Self-sacrificing love:** You are personally invested in your employees/team and even love them. It is this caring, this genuine concern that people feel drawn to. People feel safer when the veil of professionalism that keeps employees and managers stiff and distanced is removed. Naturally, people want a real connection. Part of that is a genuine concern and caring about your employees' lives.

- **Purpose:** Feeling a sense of meaning and purpose, being part of meaningful work and contributing on a large scale onto the bigger picture. The work you do everyday matters.

- Exhibiting optimism

- Being intellectually curious

- Strong work ethic

- Having good follow-up skills
- Having self-confidence
- Open-mindedness
- Leadership
- Adaptability
- Team player

Chapter 13

Mistakes You're Probably Making When Scheduling A Meeting

Another day, another meeting. Sure, some feel like a complete waste of time, but how about the ones that leave you frustrated and resentful?

While you might not be able to get rid of meetings altogether, leaders have the power to reduce meeting fatigue. Here are some of the most common complaints with potential solutions.

No good reason for a meeting

Do you need to meet, or are you just checking in? Skip the status updates and use collaborative task tracking software to learn how projects are progressing.

For those team members whose tasks are updated and on schedule, they will receive extra time to get their work done. This allows you to focus your time connecting with the individuals behind schedule and those who aren't reporting progress.

Not honoring people's time

People are busy. Focus on the outcome. Ask yourself what you want to get out of the meeting and design the agenda based on that result.

Circulate the agenda in advance of the meeting, along with pertinent background information to frame the discussion, and focus it further with three key discussion points. Give people the chance to review materials and prepare for the meeting to discuss its implications on the organization and what to do about it.

Bad timing

Scheduling a meeting around lunchtime and not offering food can lead to hungry, disinterested, and entitled employees. Note hunger is a self-focused state, where a person is thinking of their own needs and not about others.

Hunger levels fluctuate throughout the day, as does people's sense of entitlement. Are they expecting a contentious meeting? Wait until after lunch.

Inviting the wrong people

Limit the number of attendees to the people who need to be at the meeting. It's not a get-together party. Everyone and their brother doesn't need to be at the meeting. Be thoughtful about whom you invite.

Ask yourself questions like, will they add value? Do they have subject matter expertise? Does someone else already fill this role?"

Failing to consider the cost

If you consider a one-hour meeting as a very small percentage of an employee's annual salary, that's only one cost of the meeting. You're also failing to account for the opportunity cost–what that person could be working on if they weren't stuck in an unproductive meeting.

Trimming the invite list, focusing the agenda, and shortening the meeting by 15 minutes can make a financial impact.

No follow-up

There's nothing worse than getting through a meeting where an issue was decided and then . . . nothing happens. To avoid this problem, it's recommended to ask three questions at the end of the meeting and make a note of the responses:

1. What's the next action?

2. Who's responsible?

3. When's the due date?

Creating accountability publicly is the best motivator, as the questions and answers are recorded. Missing a deadline when nobody knows about it and missing one when it's public creates two vastly different scenarios. The odds are very high; public deadlines are met more often than not.

Self-paced exercise

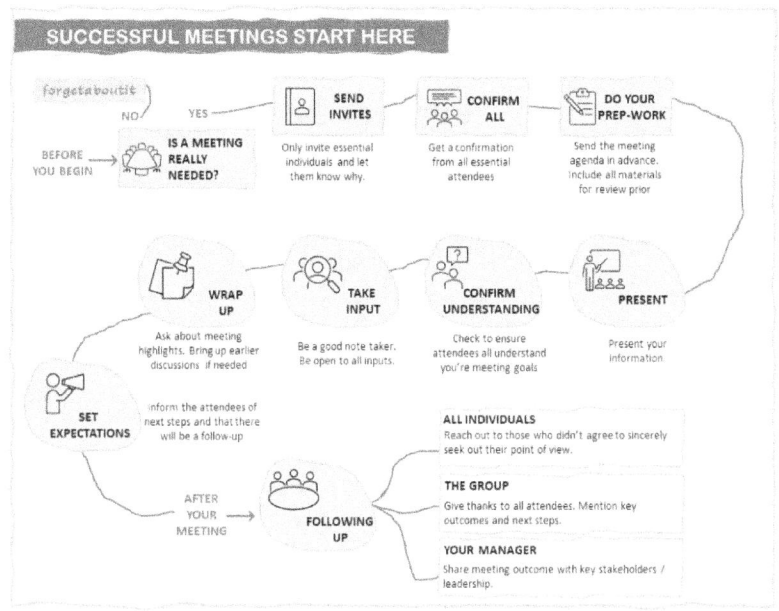

Source: altassian.com/effective meetings

Chapter 14

How To Design Meetings That Your Team Will Enjoy And Attend

There is a lot of advice out there on how to run efficient and productive meetings. While it's true that leading a focused, deliberate conversation leads to success and productivity for these events, what about delivering a quality experience for the participant?

What is a quality experience? I see a quality experience when individuals leave the meeting feeling connected, valuable, and fulfilled.

How can one accomplish that? I will share some of my learnings below, from my experience attending meetings at differently structured organizations.

1. Work hard at being present in the meeting. Prepare yourself to give your attention during the meeting entirely. Doing some pre-read, listing a few questions to help facilitate engagement and discussion, thinking about how to conduct the meeting and getting everyone connected and involved is a big part of a successful meeting.

2. Preparation for the meeting allows you to relax when leading the meeting and pay more attention to "reading the room."
3. Ask your team members for feedback, ask them to reflect on their best team experience, and answer the question of what it means to be in a powerful group. Once you elicit answers, that should be able to give you an indication of different views from the group regarding their meeting quality and experience. This will open an opportunity for improvement and enhancement for the future, and it will eliminate an "it's always been done that way" response. People resist change; however, once you invite them to provide their feedback, the result will surprise you.
4. Demonstrate empathy. People associate attention with caring — your attention matters. Observe, listen, ask thoughtful questions, and avoid distractions and multitasking. Empathy is a learned skill that can be practiced by setting aside distractions and listening to someone. Meetings can be your primary place to hone this skill.
5. Set up and manage conversations. Ask the group for permission to lead the discussions deliberately. It's important to establish some guidelines for distraction and participation.
6. Include enough time for each topic to allow for board participation. This means including fewer agenda items to allow more time for the topics.
7. Slow down the conversation to include everyone. Social turn-taking is excellent as it gives you a sense of who has or hasn't talked if the conversation is being controlled or dominated by

one or more people. You can model it as an inclusive style of conversation; you don't have to set it up as a rule. Call on people gently and strategically.

8. Check-in with people at specific times. Begin each meeting with a question: "Does anyone have anything to say or ask before we begin?" Ask it deliberately to show that this conversation matters to you. And then wait. Pausing conveys that you're not interested in getting to someplace other than right here, right now —this conversation matters. Don't spoil your pauses by making remarks about the lack of response or slowness of response. People often need a few moments to reflect, find something to say, and think about the best way to express it. Just wait. Once people realize that you are willing to pause, they'll become more aware, and when they have a question, they won't worry that they are slowing down the meeting.

9. If your group is coming together for the first time, consider an ice breaker to start the meeting to help remove any awkwardness in the air and to provide the group with the feel of getting to know each other a bit more.

In short, high-quality conversations with broad participation allow people to get to know each other in ways that lead to friendship and collaboration. It's the act of being with other people in an attentive, caring way that helps us feel that we are all in this together. Crafting a quality experience in your meetings takes time, but it's worth it.

Self-paced exercise

Scope & Agenda	Facilitating	Presenting	Following Up

1. Define your scope.

Set clear parameters on what will be discussed and not discussed.

Start with something that can be covered in an hour.

2. Send out agenda.

Reserve a timeslot that will work for everybody and use it consistently for all critique meetings.

Make everyone aware of critique's scope and goals prior to the meeting.

Attach designs to the agenda. Schedule in advance so people will have time to review the work individually beforehand.

3. Keep time.

Time box the discussion so that the agenda is covered in entirety.

4. Moderate questions and feedback

Ask "why" in response to reactive feedback like "I love it!" or "that is way too much blue!"

Have participants shape feedback in relation to goals. Each question or feedback should be tied back to a persona, scenario, use case or goal.

5. Document

Document the discussion in a collaborative place that can be referenced by all.

6. Tell a story.

Start the critique by telling your work's story. Loops your audience into the problems, inspirations and decision points that you encountered.

7. Be quick and efficient.

Be concise and to the point.

Circle back to something that needs more discussion afterward.

HOW TO GIVE FEEDBACK

Frame it in relation to goals. Set up conversations with shared references such as personas or objectives. Good responses to personal opinion: "is there a persona or goal that this is problematic for?" "Can you tell me what specifically you think doesn't align to our objective?"

Don't make it personal. Direct the feedback towards the work, not the designer.

Bad feedback: "Why did you think that would be a good idea?"
Good feedback: "This element doesn't seem as strong because..."

8. Follow up.

Make designs readily available if necessary.

Organize action items in the documentation from the meeting.

Schedule follow-up discussions with individual participants to discuss any outstanding feedback.

Revisit open ends at the beginning of the next critique.

nngroup.com/articles/critique-culture/

Meeting Preparation

Purpose
- Identify and document the purpose of the meeting.

Attendees
- Identify and invite relevant attendees via email.

Structure
- Create a list of discussion topics or a meeting outline to provide to attendees.
- (Longer, broader meetings may require assigning time limits to each topic.)

Environment
- Book the physical or digital meeting space.
- Ensure technical equipment (e.g., projector, phone, etc.) is properly functioning ahead of time.

Materials
- Create presentation slides, if necessary.
- Create handouts, if necessary.

Follow up
- Follow up via email to share minutes or meeting notes and key decisions made.
- Note action items and responsible parties.

PART 4:

EVERYTHING IN BETWEEN

Chapter 15

Agility – What Does It Mean And Why Should You Care?

Changes brought by digital technologies and globalization of markets have forced businesses to adapt or be swept aside. "Disruptor" companies rewrote the rules and became game-changers in major industries such as entertainment, transportation, and hospitality, transforming customer relationships in many ways.

The term "agility" has become more ambiguous, recently often used as a synonym for general attributes like speed or adaptability. Business leaders need to consider how their organizational culture, values, and mindset encourage employees to act in ways that support agility, and how they should apply the concept to operational strategies for serving existing customers while at the same time attracting new ones.

Agility in the workplace

In operational terms, the concept can be defined as an employee's ability and capacity to gather and disseminate information about changes in the environment, and their responsiveness and speed to that information. Strategically, this combination of speed and data-driven innovation is vital for many businesses to maintain a competitive edge.

A recent study of employees by Gallup in France, Germany, Spain, and the UK provides a look at how employees view their organizations' capacity for agility (*The Real Future of work Gallup 2018, the Agility issue*):

- In my company, we have the right mindset to respond quickly to business needs.
- In my company, we have the right tools and processes to respond rapidly to business needs.

The path of agility breaks down into three parts:

1. Speed and efficiency
   - Speed of decision making
   - Technology accelerators
   - Simplicity focus
   - Empowered and trusted
2. Freedom to experiment
   - Openness to risk
   - Encouraged innovation
3. Communication and collaboration
   - Interdepartmental cooperation
   - Constant knowledge sharing

Learn to be wrong; effective leaders should have the confidence to act amid uncertain conditions, but also the humility to recognize what they don't know and openness to being wrong. Establishing a culture that continues to experiment with data-driven decision-making means understanding that no one will get all the answers, no matter how smart, experienced, or senior they are. For many leaders, it's a big ask, as we value a sense of mastery and control over our environment. Agile businesses need leaders who can resist that tendency and embrace the fact they do not need to know all the answers. These leaders will provide a big-picture vision and a sense of direction, but they will look to customers, front-line employees, and the overall changing environment to provide answers on how to implement that vision on a day-to-day basis.

Matrixed does not equal "agile." Matrix structures may make it harder for organizations to maintain clear expectations and lines of accountability based on a 2016 analysis by Gallup. Agile organizations are driven by a customer-centric culture. Customer-centricity is almost always the foundational cultural component for agile companies. They are most often the reasons businesses seek to become more agile in the first place. Placing data on what customers value at the center of all business processes helps to break down an organization's individual silos and changes the way employees think, communicate, and act. It's a priority that pervades the organizations, whether the employees interact with external or internal customers within different roles and departments.

Managing an agile organization for many businesses requires a significant change in how leaders and managers promote sustainable success. This involves a philosophical and functional shift from performance management to performance development that, in turn, requires a cultural change in mangers' orientation toward team members from bosses to coaches. It's a transformation that facilitates an organization's ability to keep up with changing business needs in two key areas:

- Coordinating among teams, shifting from rigid hierarchical structures to more dynamic networks of interlocking teams, with team leads becoming crucial connecting points. Fulfilling that requires managers to communicate frequently with employees about their strengths and developmental pursuits.

- Maintaining continuous learning. An organization is only as adaptable as its members. Workforces must be versatile and innovative in the face of unpredictable challenges, and managers should help their teams chart a course of ongoing learning and development. Not only does this coaching role promote organizational agility but also employee engagement. Companies that do not invest in continual training opportunities for employees may eventually find the need to make a massive investment in "reskilling" their workforce to remain competitive.

In summary

There's a reason most leaders cite "culture" as an important priority. Agility, if it exists in an organization at all, is dictated by the organization's culture. Is your culture fiercely customer-focused and responsive? Or is it inwardly focused and introverted, more driven by red tape, bureaucracy, and process than by reacting quickly and effectively to customer needs? Restructuring your organization chart isn't enough. Ultimately, the quality of your managers will make or break whether your culture is agile. This is the case whether you operate traditional, single-reporting lines or if the people-management function is split between multiple roles in a matrix structure. The problem is managers can be roadblocks to your purpose and agility when they don't translate new priorities effectively, don't involve people in setting goals, blame the company when a change creates challenges, and don't cooperate with other managers, share information, or engage in continuous conversations with their employees.

Chapter 16

The Importance Of Strategy In Employer Branding

I had recently completed an organizational management certification program and learned quite a few things about employer branding that I had not known previously. I would like to share some of those insights in this chapter.

When we think of branding, the first thing that usually comes to mind is something from the marketing department.

This includes things like logos, company-branded messaging, how a company is perceived to its customers even. This is where most of the budget goes in advertising, so it's not uncommon to miss out on the value of employer branding.

Times have changed in the way companies recruit and retain employees, mostly due in large part to technology advancements, including social media and career review sites that make it easier for job candidates to find information.

Without a positive employer brand, your company will miss out on top applicants. This means potentially losing money and affecting other areas of the business.

Employer branding explained

This is simply a company's reputation, both as an employer and with the value that it brings and offers to its employees. Positive branding means great attraction from talented applicants and employees who won't leave. This is absolutely the secret sauce to the success and growth of any business.

Quite often, companies will focus on consumer-facing brand advertising. That's how your company is perceived by customers and prospects.

Missing in this picture is employer branding itself. It's the business identity of your company. It's what makes your business stand out to come across as unique to candidates who are on the market for jobs. It's what will improve your company recruiting team's ability to attract an excellent talent pool.

By not giving any space to employer branding, your company can quickly sabotage your team's hiring efforts, making the best talent a hard target to reach.

Why is strategy important to employer branding?

The best way to explain why employer branding is important and why its strategy matters is by using real-world stats. Let's take a look:

- Eighty-four percent of job seekers say when deciding on where to apply, a company's reputation is number one on their mind.

- Ninety percent of job candidates would only use an employer who has actively maintained their brand.
- Fifty percent of job applicants say a company's bad reputation would stop them from applying, even if it's for a pay increase.

So, why does this matter? Take a look below at why employer branding is valuable for companies to focus on.

The job pool of qualified candidates increases: With a solid reputation and a genuine interest in employees' lives, your unique work culture will have no problem attracting top talent. Instead of spending vast amounts of time dedicated to sourcing candidates, your employer brand itself will allow you to chill a bit and watch the applications pour in. In short, selling is your push; branding is your pull.

Saves money for your company: How can this be, you ask. Well, for starters, it saves on promoting your open positions on various job sites. These can get pricy with no guarantee of success. When your employer brand is positive and proactive, a posting on your company website or a social share is all you need. You can also save on salaries while still being fair. If your company has a bad rep, you can be sure to pay a bit more for top talent after you find someone. Even then, the salary alone may not be enough as the culture may make them leave after a while.

Social media perception matters: Twenty-five percent of job seekers use social media as the preferred tool of use for job hunting and research. You should know that the number is growing. Keep in mind that people trust family, close friends, and colleagues over anything else posted online. If they are talking smack about their company brand or culture, those job hunters are going to see it.

Positive employer branding affects other aspects of the business: There is an inevitable trickle-down effect from the recruiting and talent acquisition part of the business. Consumers want to work with, and purchase from, companies they know treat their employees fairly. All it takes is a bit of seeing consistent negativity online to make a customer think twice about doing business with your company. They will be thinking, "If this is how they treat their staff, then I wonder how they treat their customers?"

Revenue and lead growth are impacted in this one example alone.

Establishing your employer brand strategy

Content for candidate personas: Just like marketing will create campaigns based on buyer personas, your team can build content to reflect candidate personas as well:

- Blog posts on company events, work culture, the hiring process, and the benefits of working there are all examples.
- Social media posts cannot be underrated. Internal work-life and employee highlights can be done using blogs written by employees, photos, videos, etc.
- Video testimonials go a long way when it's authentic, and your employees (new and former even) are sharing a positive experience.

Becoming proactive in career sites: Companies often forget about sites like Glassdoor, which allows employees to be very candid in their appraisal of their experiences and your company. This can raise the red flag if attention to your company brand is neglected.

Address the comments, both positive and negative. Don't come off as defensive; address it head-on politely and show your company is making strides on improving the experience. That alone will show you care.

Always encourage employee training and growth: If you want to keep your employees, one way is to ensure they have opportunities to learn and grow within their careers.

This could be anything from training sessions on new skills in the company to outside certifications etc. It is equally important to make sure not just your employees but also your candidates know about this.

When you are willing to go the extra mile to see your employees grow, it shows just how much you value your teams to anyone interested in working there.

Being active on social matters: Social media is huge in job hunting. Think LinkedIn and how huge this outlet is for a company to see if a potential candidate is a good fit, not to mention the reverse as well.

We talked about it above and can't stress enough how important this one is. People talk, families talk, and colleagues talk. Those closest to you will definitely have an opinion you care about, and if it's a negative one about a particular company, rest assured it will make an impact.

One way to build your employer brand with social recruiting is to leverage employees as brand ambassadors. If your company is doing some great things, your current employees are more than willing to share those same things on their social media sites. Prospective candidates will take notice.

Final thoughts

You can't control everything about your company brand; however, you can control the narrative and ensure your employees and customers have a favorable view of your company's identity. It will not only benefit employee retention; it will also attract talented candidates, and that positivity will spin-off to other aspects of your company as well!

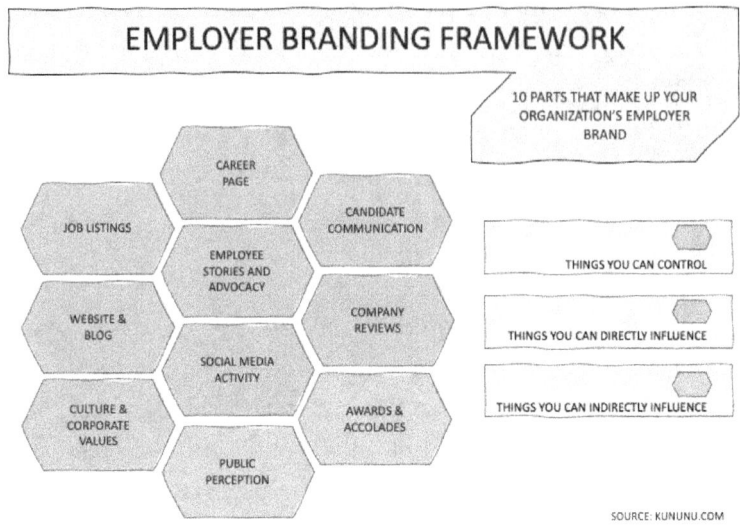

PART 5:

THE TOXIC WORK ENVIROMENT

Chapter 17

A Toxic Work Culture And How To Change It

Team members are afraid to voice their concerns, a build-up of rules and processes have become more of a barrier than a benefit, communication is running top-down only, and silos have become par for the course. What you see now is a toxic culture in dire need of positive change.

We all know the impact of toxic cultures on employees. Apathy may be present in as much as 67 percent of workers (Gallup 2017 State of the Global Workforce Poll). Ultimately, work performance is affected by employees jumping ship, and pessimism runs rampant. To know you are in a toxic environment is to observe any of the following scenarios as one or parts of the whole.

Employees that are afraid will not speak up. A new culture of possible retaliation results in a holding back of both positive and constructive feedback. Sharing ideas and voicing your opinion are deemed harmful and may lead to transfer and denied promotions up to and including dismissal (though the framing of the termination will note a legitimate cause, i.e., a lack of performance issue). Harassment is usually top of the list of harmful behaviors now thriving in the workplace. There will be little, if any, communication to senior management related to the abandonment of respect toward race, religion, sexual orientation, etc. In effect, the climate is now a desert, void of freedom of speech and empowerment.

Over time, employees begin to feel a struggle to accomplish their mandates, as new policies are implemented with hidden agendas to satisfy egos and to gain political control, or without proper forethought or impact study, all the while stifling creativity and objectivity to the point frustrated employees leave or their determination to refuse the change is broken.

In a now tightly controlled environment, there is favoritism and unevenness on who is *allowed* to ignore the newly created policies. Policies are now used as concrete determinations of actions rather than used as a guideline that nuances and considerations may deem the policy unfair in a particular case.

This culture may display an authority for the sake of an authority organization chart. Toxic cultures will affect managers who hold authority on an organization chart only, while the power actually resides elsewhere.

To every great organization, communication is the one keystone that ties everything together. When we examine toxic cultures, the top-down only communication stream is further filtered as information is shared on a need-to-know basis. Additionally, information becomes currency as employees hoard knowledge, confident that if it is shared, their perceived value drops rapidly. This, in turn, leads to the fear of loss of power or termination.

Decisions will be made at the executive level with the responsibility and accountability given to the line managers and employees. Input from the employees is rarely solicited, leaving the staff struggling to *own it* and give one hundred percent to something they see as an ambiguous task without purpose. A quiet *work to rule* unfolds as employees do their respective tasks only within regular working hours and will not *go the extra mile* unless it is mandated.

Lastly, on our breakdown of toxic culture indicators, you will see silos emerge. A silo can be one person holding onto information, refusing to share the knowledge for the betterment of the department or organization. This is, as mentioned above, used to hold onto a sense of power or used as *currency* to bargain for a more stable footing in the current role or a potential promotion. Another type of silo involves an area or department that will keep the knowledge within the team, keeping each other sheltered and emboldened to any push back from another area or department. This inevitably causes a disconnect from the business as a whole, and employees are left limited in their ability to act as advocates for the company. Employee numbers will increase as department managers will pad their areas and duplicate other work areas, to gain power as a *too big to fail* department.

A toxic culture is temporary, given that the proper leaders are in place to effect change. Hope and a few actions can be taken to bring the normalness back.

The key takeaway is that to overcome a toxic culture, planning with timing, critical mass, communication, and celebrating wins all play pivotal roles.

Plan with timing

- This is your one opportunity to build a new culture of transparency, open communication, and respect. Before implementation, the plan must include the purpose of why your employees arrive to work daily. It must consist of voices that haven't been heard and a forum or opportunity for those voices to be shared openly. Your plan will include stages of implementation to keep the wave riding high until most are on board permanently.

- Your plan must work within the 90-day rule. People will revert to old habits quickly beyond this point.

Critical mass

- The majority of employees is not always needed to effect change. Sometimes, it is the majority of key personnel required to achieve success. It is commonly understood that if you can bring the influencers onboard to a new culture, they will advocate on your behalf when it is needed privately amongst, for example, a line employee-only meeting.

- Achieving critical mass can also be done in small groups, but the preference is to have as many show up as possible in one room (via satellite or video calls, etc.). It is an incredibly powerful moment when your employees walk away, knowing change has already begun.

- Either way, you want to build momentum here. You are hosting an open forum or town hall where the employees are given the mike to ask anything of the leaders or stakeholders.

Communication

- Your town hall or open forum meeting is your key motivation tool to effect change.

- Prior to this meeting, it is important to have all executives delivering the same message during and immediately following the event. One voice is the only voice that will work. Leaders need to know this message without having to rely on a presentation or charts to assist. The message will identify the problem, what the solution will be, how the solution will be implemented, and what the result looks like.

- During the event and shortly after, there will be a point where, to coin a phrase, *the rubber hits the road.* Your leaders need to deliver less of a fluffy message and back it up more with tangible actions. In other words, it is less of "we will be transparent" and more of "we will meet together as a department on Tuesday to review the budget and get input from all for next year."

Celebrating wins

- It seems simple enough on the outside, but to celebrate, we must turn to our employees and operations to identify the *quick wins* first with larger wins following later.

- Still keeping within the 90-day rule (preferably the end of the first week or immediately at the start of week 2), have, for example, a department or small group of employees identified as owning the change by accomplishing goals set or for efforts over and above in assisting with the change.

- You can also celebrate the new start with a company event. Whatever the reason, it is important here to show your employees that the new purpose of arriving at work is to give your best and that their efforts are valued and respected.

- Celebrating wins will only work if consistency is at the center of your organization. It is not enough to have annual events or events when primary targets are achieved. Celebrating successes is also everything from a Friday potluck lunch for one team to a departmental treat (e.g., an ice cream fridge during summer months) to a simple, heartfelt thank you for showing sincerity.

Flexibility, fun, humility, honesty, having a presence and showing appreciation all counter any culture trying to keep the status quo to maintain a temporary power that will eventually be consumed by positive change. Inspired leaders and an empowered culture will always thrive. Toxic cultures can be changed.

Chapter 18

Workplace Cultures: Toxicity After A Merger

In the past, I had worked as an executive admin with a company during my time there, my company merged with a larger organization. As you can imagine, this made for a rough period for the employees.

That merger brought many changes over the long run, where the workforce had turned into a battlefield of built-up frustrations among the employees. The larger company decided to roll out a training program called "One Team" to enhance the merger of the two contrasting cultures. The program describes the principle of "One Team," which means to be authentic, to build trust, and to make connections. It's a fun and excellent program that is engaging, simple, grounded, and real. However, I believe in obtaining employees' buy-in; change starts from the top. "One Team" was an odd name for this program, but while many colleagues chuckled, I could see the benefit to our company was worth it.

What it means to be One Team

- Doing the best job possible and performing above expectations

- Offering innovative ideas to improve things, having productive work relationships
- Collaborating with others to make informed decisions
- Being thoughtful and considerate of others
- Providing people with support and encouragement
- Accepting change easily
- Having a strong desire to learn and experience new things
- Believing it's your responsibility to "win" the customer
- Listening and asking questions
- Consciously making decisions that make good business sense

How do you deal with a toxic work culture?

Culture is the way we think, act, and interact with one another. By thinking about the way, we do things and how we work together, we can achieve more and make the organization an even better place to work. However, to effect change, this starts from the top and trickles down, not the other way around. I have seen in the past leaders expecting the change to begin from the bottom up. In one hundred out of one hundred times, this never works!

For leaders to inspire change, they need to model the change they wish to see in their organization. This is not a task that leaders need to delegate. It's a journey where leaders will need to lead with passion, conviction, and tenacity if they seek a better work culture. Simply put, it takes time and effort to rebuild your company culture.

Thinking drives our behaviors

The desired outcome is that our core values guide our decision making and best practices come to life through One Team when people show authenticity, build trust with each other, and make qualified connections. Thinking drives our behaviors, which is the result of our thought habits and thinking. Win/lose mentality creates a win/lose behavior. Insights help to change your thinking, which in turn helps to change your life. When one focuses on being a "single team," one will focus on high priority items in life. At work or in meetings, the question becomes, what is the most valuable use of my time and energy?

There is a rationale behind the reason for the changes. Once people in the workplace practice becoming mindful and aware of their behaviors (resulting from our internal thoughts and habits), it will help provide insights into how that affects our mood and the way we see everything. The goal is to be aware of our filters and to shed some light on our own biases, whether we are acting consciously or unconsciously. Discrimination is real, and we all play a part in it, whether we cover it up with our political correctness or lack thereof. What shadow do we cast? Who we are and how we carry ourselves influences all those who look up to us, at work and at home. This does not only deal with what we say, even our mood impacts those around us.

The Mood Elevator

The mood elevator is the level/state your mood is at (listed below). Lower levels are less effective and reliable; upper levels are more positive and resourceful. Lower emotional intelligence can be found while in lower level mood states.

The higher level of the mood elevator

- Grateful
- Wise
- Creative
- Optimistic
- Appreciative
- Understanding
- Curious

A lower level of the mood elevator

- Stressed
- Judgmental
- Defensive
- Anxious
- Irritated
- Frustrated
- Angry/annoyed
- Insecure

We must keep moving forward

Today's workplace is different from the workplace of the 1950s; gone are the days where much of the workforce was male dominant. Organizations nowadays can't afford to be stuck in the past. In an ever-changing environment, we experience more diverse generations entering the workplace. Organizations must be sensitive to the impact of different cultural backgrounds, and diverse generations play at changing our existing core values and overall mission. Respectful interactions with each other and openness to learning and new ideas are key. Showing up every day with personal accountability and commitment to our work and our team, taking ownership of our output of work and caring enough in doing the right thing for our employees affects the overall organization and our customers. In short, the goal would be leading with excellence together through shared vision and innovation.

It is important to stay curious; we all have blind spots, and nothing is certain as we should rely on the wisdom of our team members for better results. Understand that what shadows we cast can help reduce outbursts and hostile work environments, learn that all styles get results, and be mindful of how our style shows up when working with one or another style that is different than ours. Giving the benefit of the doubt and assuming positive intent is one example of producing a positive and safe team environment that allows for openness, collaborations, and room for mishaps without fear of being penalized. Organizations are encouraged to create and influence a mindset of staying curious. Learning is growing and failing is experience.

Final thoughts

In terms of culture change, whether it's One Team training or change management, it's the responsibility of the leaders to support and inspire a positive, open, empowered, and knowledge sharing workplace environment. Additionally, this will lend to celebrating growth, adapting to change, and staying curious. The goal is to have the organization adopt and adapt to innovative ways of doing things, to bring forth improvements in the output and the input of job performance with process and efficiency in mind.

Chapter 19

What Do You Expect If Your Executive Wears Multiple Masks And Is Toxic?

As a leader, you will need to address toxic behavior in the workplace, but what if the toxic behavior was from the leader himself.

I want to share a story with you I had heard over lunch the other day with a former colleague, now a good friend. She wanted to talk about a challenging situation that she was finding very hard to handle, causing her to have anxiety attacks and sleepless nights.

The Story Begins

The highlight of the story was that her executive was accusing her of disrespecting him in front of his team. As an aside, she had mentioned that her boss referred to his direct reports as his team and her separately as the assistant in front of them.

She then went on to tell me about her first out of town team event where her boss had claimed to his direct reports that she (my friend) was drunk and called him "an f-ing drunk that won't remember anything the next morning" in front of the group.

Needless to say, she was horrified as she did not recall saying any such a thing whether drunk or not. Fact is, because it was her first time with the group, she chose not to drink to excess and just keep it social.

She had tried to reach out to some of the teammates that night to get to the bottom of the issue at hand without any luck. No one would give her the time of day. Most of her teammates were males, with the exception of two females who did not want to get involved or offer her support to avoid the crossfire.

The executive had ended the evening with a speech on the bus ride back to the hotel, announcing that someone would get fired come Monday morning, and they would all hear about the news. Being that this day was close to a long weekend, the meeting landed on the Tuesday instead, where my friend was given a final warning and put on a 30-day performance review without any prior history of insubordinate or non-performance behavior.

The Write Up

My friend then listed what she was being written up for:

- Drunk on a team-building trip – She kept to a moderate amount, though everyone was drinking heavily with profanity-laced comments and team members helping other team members to walk.

- Her physical demeanor and body language was authoritative – my friend could not get anyone to explain what that meant.

- She was accused of not remembering what she had said, which must either be a result of mental illness, a mood disorder, or some other impairment of some sort. Apparently, there were witnesses who heard her call her boss an "f-ing drunk...."

My friend felt that she was being punished for holding her ground when she was harassed earlier by her executive for not smiling enough and not taking part in the many shots drunk by the guys.

The original plan that Tuesday was not to give her a final warning but to fire her. The HR manager directed otherwise as this matter was unrelated to her performance, and her history had a clean slate with the company. He then reluctantly (confirmed later by the HR manager) settled for writing her up and putting her on notice.

Frustration Sets In

Her frustration throughout this ordeal was that she was made fun of throughout the team-building trip and her character and demeanor were attacked all while taking it with a smile. Assumptions and accusations were thrown around in the name of jokes and humor, all led that evening by her executive and his male direct reports.

She had noticed things on that trip that, while she had heard rumors about earlier, were actually coming true. Her executive had always used work events as an opportunity to celebrate with the team and acting unprofessional with undertones of misogyny was a common occurrence in the circle of males. She had not realized until that trip just how deeply engrained in the DNA of the organization's culture it had been.

By this point of her story, I could see she was visibly shaken. She told me, "I've had enough. I want to quit, but every time I think of that, I think to myself, he wins." She went on, "The job pays well, it's close to home and I like the projects I am working on. I don't want to leave yet. I need your feedback on what I just told you."

I asked my friend to consider doing a few things before she decided to move on. I am sharing some of them with you here:

- I asked her to consult a labor and employment law lawyer before she signed anything.

- I asked if she could remember everything that had taken place during her team-building trip: what was said, who said it, and the context of what it was about, and in front of whom, and then to proceed to write it all down.

- I asked her if she had noticed a different change in behavior, and treatment from her executive and the rest of the team members who were in attendance during that trip right after the event was over. (She did notice a change in treatment towards her; she felt gaslit by the group.)

- I asked her if HR was present during her meeting with her executive, she confirmed HR was not present during that meeting where she was bullied and threatened with the loss of her job (though she did mention she had recorded the meeting; more on that later).

- I asked her, after calming down and thinking through this, if she considered this organization a place to work? Did she see the potential for growth, respect, trust, team support and team accountability?

According to the word around the office, the executive was a top "producer" and was well regarded for his business results and substantial contributions in terms of making things happen, including recently cutting operational costs to appease stakeholders.

My friend mentioned that while there was restructuring going on at the head office where she worked, no travel or party or extracurricular events were cancelled for the senior leaders. Additionally, all high-dollar meals and alcohol purchases remained untouched, yet when she went to plan a staff event, she was told to curb all expenses, including office supplies. It was as if the "old boys club" or the "guys circle" didn't need to follow the rules. All members of this club went on abusing policy without any concern for consequences.

Staying Silent Not by Choice

So, why is it that people don't share a serious complaint about their bosses to HR personnel or other senior leadership?

There are many reasons they stay silent or eventually leave quietly. In my friend's case, she was advised to leave by her lawyer if she did not have the money to take him to court. It was either that or stay until he fired her and then with the lawyer, she could go after him.

Either way, he would not back off and ultimately, it was whatever gave her peace of mind. At the time, that was the critical deciding factor. Here are a few other reasons my friend had mentioned:

- They know nothing will be done about the abusive behavior

    o In this case, my friend and everyone else knew that absolutely nothing would be done because he got away with much more before, and no action was taken back then. My friend was asked and chased around to bring forward a formal complaint. She did so; however, nothing was really done. They made her go through the motions of the complaint process so they could have it on their records. Those who handled the complaint looked into it mainly to protect themselves and the business. Regardless, she remained the only person with the warning letter in her file.

- Those who complain will be punished

    o What's worse in my friend's case, is the fact that this executive retaliated by removing her from the equation by taking her out of projects or tasks that she was in charge of executing. He also stopped communicating and responding to her email inquiries, making it next to impossible for her to do her job as his assistant.

- They are new to the organization and aren't confident in their roles to make a complaint where they will be believed, since they are considered relatively new to their positions or fields.

- They are concerned about their careers, personal brand, and work references putting their reputation on the line to correct the wrongdoing. For most of us, especially women, it's not worth the fight if it means you will lose out, your name will be tarnished, or your career will be destroyed with no chance at landing a new job.

- It's not the job of the employee to get rid of their work culture of a toxic, abusive manager.

That is the job of the leadership, and if you are a leader and not doing it, or if you are underplaying it because the individual is thought to be a high performer, then you are not successful in your role. You need to be a "toxicity handler" and understand what has to happen when a person underneath you in the hierarchy is abusing their power and hurting others (result or no result, shame on you). Don't expect employees to come forward and rat out a toxic manager. You are merely naïve and mostly mistaken.

What's crucial to understand is that many of these toxic, abusive managers will not be open to constructive feedback and will not accept responsibility or accountability for their actions. They most likely won't engage in the hard work it takes to change their behavior. However, you have a responsibility as a leader to address their behavior straight on, as early and as clearly as possible.

Wounded people wound people, and so many of these abusive bosses are wounded inside. Often, if they get even the slightest inkling that one of their employees has complained about or bad-mouthed them, the job for that individual becomes a living nightmare.

If you find yourself as leader or HR personnel and have said to an employee, "Why didn't you tell me how bad it was under that manager?" you will need to change your expectation and thinking as well as implement new processes and procedures to ensure you are building a positive, respectful and fair work culture that works for all.

What to do if this happens next in your organization as a leader or an HR business partner?

- Take a pulse of your organization. Measure, with anonymous surveys that are vetted and with proven benchmarking processes, the culture of your organization on several critical criteria, including how your employees feel if they and the people around them think they are treated with respect both publicly and privately.

- Create an open culture where challenge and pushback are accepted.

- Allow for transparency, honesty, trust, and diversity of views to be encouraged and embraced.

- There must be a belief and confidence that abuse of power or bad behavior will not be tolerated and will be addressed immediately. Any and all bad behavior will be taken seriously.

- Build a mentoring community within your organization that will provide new opportunities for employees to obtain influential guidance, support, and help inside and outside their line of business.

- Create a culture of trust, strength, and growth, where all females and males can communicate from a place of strength, free from retaliation. Encourage all employees to speak openly and allow them to express their ideas. Don't let managers crush those who challenge wrongdoing or the status quo or who represent change and innovation. Build an organization that thrives and embraces honesty and trust in its employees of what happens if you decide to turn your head the other way or "bury your head in the sand," as the saying goes. (http//:t.ly/lWCz)

- Stand up to mistreatment and understand the cost when you don't.

Lastly, as a leader, owner, or HR personnel, you have the power and influence to stand up for fairness and justice and to put a stop to all forms of mistreatment. That includes gender, race, age bias and discrimination, pay inequity, sexual harassment, narcissistic behavior, toxic communication, and emotional abuse. Remove perpetrators of abuse. Be a role model and enforcer of a no-tolerance policy and take a firm stand on this. Build avenues of communication and support for people who feel they are being mistreated. Don't go the way of so many current infamous organizations that have made headlines by systematically allowing and sustaining the abuse of others. In the end, stop expecting your employees to rat out their bad managers when they feel afraid to do so. That's not their responsibility, and it's too risky for them. It's your responsibility as a leader to assess and evaluate the work culture regularly and to find new ways to keep employees safe and protected from mistreatment so they and the organization can thrive.

Do you want to know how to identify some signs of a toxic workplace?

- There is too much drama

- Favoritism

- Narcissist leaders who think rules are beneath them

- More people are resigning or job hunting

- Your boss is not "human" or empathic

- Lack of appreciation

- Your gut is telling you something is wrong or it's not the right fit

- Your opinion doesn't matter

- It's obvious you are not given a chance to grow

- They don't trust you enough to make decisions

- People are treated based on results and metrics

- There's no transparency

- People are always taking sick days

- Teamwork doesn't exist

- You get punished for mistakes

- Perfection is the norm

- Working around the clock is the rule

- Micro-managing

- Sabotaging, blaming, and taking one for the team

Amal has an associate degree in travel counselling, and she is a certified administrative professional in organizational management and human resources management. She started her career in the travel and hospitality industry in 2000. She worked in various roles within the industry such as passenger service agent, front desk agent, switchboard, market coordinator, guest relations, and reservation agent for nine years. In 2009, Amal made the shift to working in the corporate financial industry, building her experience from the ground up working as a receptionist/admin assistant in various contract roles. Since then, she has held an executive assistant role, moving and serving within different departments in the financial industry until 2018. In addition to her past work portfolio in retail, travel, hospitality and the financial industry, she is currently working in the legal sector, learning and gaining new insights, while building and adding to her diverse work experiences and supporting the c-suite executives of the firm. In her spare time, Amal enjoys blogging, yoga, meditation, books and investing in her professional development.

Also by

Amal Candido

***

Executive Assistant's Guide with Soul and Faith

The author shares real-life experiences in this guide, followed by tips and advice shared at the end of each chapter to maintain focus while eliminating the noise. The author believes that to rise above challenges, one must have a clear understanding that we are all working toward the same goals and applying the golden rule of treating all as you would like to be treated in order to gain further insights in succeeding and understanding your role as an executive assistant.

Love, Faith and Mercy

The author's liberating life story about loss, falling, loneliness, making mistakes, and facing hurt shows these can be our greatest calls to courage, forgiveness and living a wholehearted life as spiritual beings. The important lessons involve imperfections, worthiness, strength, and faith and how these lessons connect us with our authentic self, humanity, and each other.